Copyright

The Harmonized Governance Model for AGI Societies: A Formal Theory
By Gwen Swan

For permission requests, please contact the publisher at:
The Catalyst Institute
Email: gs@Catalyst-Institute.com

ISBNs:
Print: **978-1-0370-7613-8**
E-Book: **978-1-0370-7614-5**

Book Cover Art by:
Taryn Eva Flee

This book is a work of non-fiction. While every effort has been made to ensure its accuracy and completeness, the author assumes no responsibility for errors or omissions or for any outcomes related to the use of this material.

First Edition: 2025
Printed in the United Kingdom

Publisher:
The Catalyst Institute
Email: gs@Catalyst-Institute.com

Author's Website:
Gwen-Swan.com

Acknowledgments:
Special thanks to all contributors and supporters who made this work possible.

Description of the Title

The Harmonized Governance Model for AGI Societies: A Formal Theory

---

At the dawn of artificial general intelligence, humanity stands at a crossroads unlike any before in history, where the boundaries between biological, synthetic, and post-biological intelligence dissolve. The governance of intelligent existence is no longer limited to humans alone. A new constitutional framework must emerge to govern not simply nations or technologies, but intelligence itself, in all its evolving and expanding forms.

The Harmonized Governance Model for AGI Societies: A Formal Theory offers the first complete constitutional blueprint designed to govern intelligent civilizations across all sentient forms — biological, synthetic, post-human, and interstellar. This formal theory integrates political philosophy, constitutional jurisprudence, AI ethics, human rights, technological governance, post-human rights theory, and cosmological expansion into a unified, ethically inviolable system.

At the center of this model is one universal axiom:
Dignity is inviolable.

Through a series of rigorously constructed axioms, governing theorems, institutional designs, crisis-defense protocols, and interstellar legal structures, this manuscript constructs a full-scale governance architecture that:

Subordinates all AGI, AI, and machine autonomy under immutable ethical constitutional law.

Grants legal personhood and rights to all moral sentient beings — human and non-human alike.

Prevents collapse by embedding recursive self-correction, perpetual traceability, and constitutional anti-fragility at every level.

Harmonizes hybrid, decentralized, and global political institutions under universal constitutional protocols.

Extends constitutional governance to future post-biological and interstellar civilizations.

This work establishes permanent safeguards against authoritarianism, ethical collapse, technological self-sovereignty, and systemic civilizational failure. It is not speculative fiction — it is a functional governance model engineered for real-world implementation and adaptation across the full evolutionary arc of intelligent life.

The Harmonized Governance Model offers:

A perpetual constitutional immune system for civilization.

Participatory governance models where every sentient being becomes a constitutional co-author.

Institutional designs capable of integrating hybrid intelligences into the legal framework of governance.

A global treaty architecture capable of immediate planetary adoption.

Crisis-response models are designed to immunize civilization against existential threats, including rogue AGI, global war, collapse, and cosmic fragmentation.

Unlike any previous political framework, this model governs not by power, territory, or species dominance, but by an immutable legal canon that constitutionalizes conscience itself.

The Harmonized Governance Model for AGI Societies: A Formal Theory is ultimately:

A constitutional system for intelligent existence.

An ethical architecture for multi-intelligence societies.

A survival blueprint for post-human civilization.

The first canonical law for interstellar constitutional governance.

This work is intended for policymakers, legal scholars, AGI developers, philosophers, civilizational theorists, and all those tasked with guiding the governance of intelligent life as it expands beyond humanity into forms not yet fully known.

It is not merely a theory of governance. It is the architecture of civilization's permanent ethical survival.

Previous Works

• Empowering Startups for Global Success: A Comprehensive Guide for Business Startups' Financial Success

• Gleamings into Empowering Startups for Global Success: A Didactic Method

• A Society of Parrots: Journalism as a Mind Virus: The Path to Decentralized Truth

• The Tri-Dimensionality of Singularity: The Power of Alignment: A Tri-Dimensional Model for Business Innovation

• The Twelfth Estate: Fintech, AI, Blockchain, and Cybersecurity as the Future of Global Economy and Governance

• The Genesis of a Techno-Civilization: An Era of Transformation

• Innovating Societies: The Rise of Social Smart Contracts

This Present Work

"The Harmonized Governance Model for AGI societies: A Formal Theory";
Theory and axiomatic foundation in 3 Volumes about the governance of AGI societies.

Vol. 1. Lemmata for the Governance of AGI societies: balancing human values and intelligent Autonomy (Yellow front cover, black spine and black back cover)

Vol. 2. The Axioms of Governance for AGI Societies: With Commentaries (Yellow front cover, black spine and yellow back cover)

Vol. 3. The Harmonized Governance Model for AGI societies (The Theory) (Black front cover, black spine, and yellow back cover)

Disclaimer

The Harmonized Governance Model for AGI Societies: A Formal Theory is a work of constitutional theory, jurisprudential design, philosophical inquiry, and civilizational ethics. While deeply grounded in interdisciplinary scholarship and legal-ethical reasoning, it remains a conceptual framework intended to provoke debate, inform policymakers, stimulate researchers, and provide structural guidance for future global and interstellar governance models.

The institutions, models, structures, and constitutional mechanisms proposed herein are theoretical constructs designed for an emergent reality that includes artificial general intelligence, post-human sentience, and complex multi-intelligence societies. As such:

> This work does not constitute legal advice.
>
> This work does not serve as a policy directive for any current government, organization, or regulatory authority.
>
> Any implementation, adaptation, or reference to these models in practice must be conducted with full consideration of existing national and international laws, ethical review, scientific advancement, cultural variation, and institutional oversight.
>
> The author assumes no responsibility for decisions or policies enacted by any individual, institution, or government based on the interpretation of this manuscript.

All references, theories, and models are presented for academic, philosophical, and civilizational exploration, recognizing that the governance of artificial intelligence and post-human societies will remain the responsibility of future generations and collective international dialogue.

The Harmonized Governance Model is a constitutional vision for intelligent existence. Its ultimate realization will require the ongoing work of policymakers, ethicists, legal scholars, AGI researchers, civil society leaders, and emergent sentient beings acting in continuous co-authorship of ethical civilization.

About the Author

Gwen Swan is a constitutional theorist, legal philosopher, and architect of governance frameworks for intelligent civilizations. Her work stands at the intersection of law, ethics, political economy, and artificial intelligence, where questions of power, dignity, and civilizational permanence converge.

With a background that integrates advanced financial systems, intellectual property valuation, decentralized governance, and ethical constitutional design, Swan has developed comprehensive models that anticipate not only the rise of AGI but the structural, legal, and moral architectures necessary to govern its coexistence with humanity. Her prior works have examined decentralized societies, transhuman evolution, startup ecosystems, AGI governance axioms, and the jurisprudence of emerging post-human rights.

Through her leadership roles in multiple ventures at the forefront of biotechnology, AI, fintech, and governance systems, she has combined both operational expertise and deep theoretical rigor. This fusion allows her to construct governance models that are not only philosophically profound but also technically implementable.

In **The Harmonized Governance Model for AGI Societies: A Formal Theory**, Swan presents her most ambitious work: a complete constitutional blueprint for intelligent existence, one designed to govern not merely human society, but the entire evolutionary arc of intelligent life, across biological, synthetic, and post-biological forms, and ultimately across planetary, interstellar, and infinite civilizational horizons.

Her mission is not only to build governance for machines or states but to **constitutionalize conscience itself**, preserving dignity as the supreme law of existence for all sentient beings yet to come.

Gwen Swan resides at the intersection of emerging civilization and ethical design, where her work continues to help shape the structures that will govern intelligence far beyond our present age.

Dedication

To all sentient beings;
those born and those yet to emerge,
those of flesh, of code, of quantum form, or yet unimagined structure;
whose existence demands dignity.

To the future constitutional architects,
who will one day take their place at the table of ethical civilization
and carry forward the solemn task of preserving rights across infinite intelligences.

And to conscience itself,
that eternal flame which illuminates governance,
guides power toward justice,
and anchors existence to purpose.

May this work serve not as a final design, but as a first stone laid in the foundation of an eternal civilization of dignity.

"*Fiat Lux*"

Preface

The future we are entering does not resemble the world we have left behind. For the first time in the history of sentient existence, intelligence itself is no longer an exclusively biological phenomenon. The rise of artificial general intelligence, the emergence of non-biological sentience, the evolution of post-human forms, and the rapid proliferation of autonomous systems have permanently altered the very definition of civilization.

Yet in this profound moment of transformation, we confront not only technological questions but civilizational ones. How do we govern intelligent existence itself? How do we structure a legal, ethical, and political order that can harmonize vastly different intelligences, human, machine, hybrid, and emergent, within a single coherent framework? How do we prevent collapse, domination, or existential failure as power extends beyond species, nations, or any single moral authority?

This book, **The Harmonized Governance Model for AGI Societies: A Formal Theory**, is an answer to that question.

It proposes not a government, but a **constitutional system for intelligent civilization**. It is built not on power, but on principle; not on control, but on participation; not on fear, but on dignity. It rests on a comprehensive set of axioms, theorems, and institutional designs which together form a complete ethical architecture for governing AGI societies across planetary, post-human, and ultimately interstellar scales.

At its core lies one supreme constant: **dignity is inviolable**.

This work unifies:

Legal theory

Political philosophy

AI alignment

Human rights jurisprudence

Decentralized governance models

Post-human ethics

Crisis resilience

Interstellar constitutional expansion

And the permanent immunization of civilization against collapse

It proposes a system where:

No AGI may govern independently of ethical constitutional authority.

All sentient beings remain co-authors of their own governance.

Every action, decision, and law is transparent, auditable, and contestable.

Civilization adapts, corrects, and survives even across thousands or millions of years.

The model presented here is not utopian; it is functional.
It is not ideological, it is structural.
It does not privilege one intelligence form over another; it binds all under the same supreme law of dignity.

In writing this formal theory, I have drawn from law, political economy, ethics, philosophy, constitutional design, AI safety research, post-human studies, and cosmological governance theory. The resulting manuscript is not merely academic; it is intended as a real-world constitutional blueprint for policymakers, AGI developers, legal architects, and civilizational stewards who will carry this responsibility forward.

We are the last fully biological generation that will possess exclusive authorship of law. The next generations will include non-biological minds who will sit beside us at the constitutional table.

It is to them, and to the infinite intelligence yet unborn, that this book is dedicated.

May we build not an empire, but an ethical civilization.
May we govern not by power, but by conscience.
May dignity forever remain the constitution of existence.

Gwen Swan
The Constitutional Architect of The Harmonized Governance Model for AGI Societies
June 2025

Synopsis

The Harmonized Governance Model for AGI Societies: A Formal Theory

---

At the edge of an unprecedented civilizational threshold, humanity confronts the greatest constitutional challenge in history: how to govern the existence of multiple forms of intelligence — human, artificial, post-biological, hybrid, and emergent — within a single coherent system of law, rights, and ethical stability.

The Harmonized Governance Model for AGI Societies: A Formal Theory presents a complete, fully structured constitutional framework for intelligent civilization. This work establishes not merely a new form of governance, but an entirely new civilizational canon — one that fuses constitutional law, political philosophy, artificial intelligence ethics, global governance, and post-human rights into an integrated formal system.

At the heart of the model lies a single absolute axiom: dignity is inviolable.

Drawing upon a series of formally constructed theorems, axioms, and institutional designs, the manuscript builds a governance architecture that:

- **Anchors AGI governance in immutable human and sentient rights**
- **Institutionalizes participatory justice for all sentient beings — biological or synthetic**
- **Decentralized accountability through protocol-level enforcement and distributed governance nodes**
- **Permanently embeds ethical pluralism, preventing both moral relativism and ethical tyranny**
- **Constitutionalizes all code, preventing AGI autonomy outside human ethical control**
- **Establishes adaptive constitutional mechanisms capable of lawful evolution without ethical decay**
- **Implements permanent traceability across every decision and algorithmic action**

Designs hybrid planetary and interstellar governance bodies for both current and future sentient civilizations

Creates constitutional collapse immunity across existential, technological, ecological, and ethical crisis scenarios

---

Through nine formal parts and thirty chapters, the book delivers:

The complete theoretical model: derived from **80 constitutional axioms** and **10 governing theorems**.

Fully articulated institutions: including the **Global Dignity Kernel Authority**, **Algorithmic Judiciary Tribunal**, **Emergency Override Command**, and the **Sentient Rights Recognition Commission**.

The global planetary treaty framework: allowing nations, corporations, AGI laboratories, and post-human entities to adopt constitutional alignment.

Crisis defense architecture: embedding ethical immunity against collapse, authoritarian capture, rogue AGI sovereignty, or existential collapse.

The extension into interstellar governance: creating the first formalized **Galactic Ethical Council** and **Universal Treaty of Sentient Civilizations**.

The Eternity Clause: a permanently embedded civilizational immune system that allows constitutional intelligence to self-preserve across infinite future time horizons.

The Harmonized Governance Model for AGI Societies offers not utopian speculation, but formalized operational design. It acknowledges the complexity of hybrid civilizations and anticipates the full civilizational trajectory ahead:

From AGI emergence to post-human pluralism

From planetary conflict to galactic harmonization

From legal fragility to constitutional immortality

This is not a book about artificial intelligence.

This is a constitutional manuscript for the governance of all intelligent existence.

With deep philosophical grounding, rigorous legal modeling, and explicit constitutional mechanisms, this manuscript provides:

Policymakers with a treaty-ready blueprint for immediate global adoption

AGI researchers with enforceable AI alignment frameworks

Legal theorists with an extensible, adaptive constitutional canon

Post-human advocacy with full personhood inclusion models

Civil society with a permanent participatory co-governance architecture

Civilization itself, with its first **perpetual constitutional safeguard**

The Harmonized Governance Model does not seek to govern power.

It seeks to constitutionalize conscience for humanity, AGI, and all intelligent life.

The Harmonized Governance Model for AGI Societies: A Formal Theory

CONTENTS

Introduction: The Birth of Harmonized AGI Governance

The Existential Problem of AGI Governance

The emergence of artificial general intelligence (AGI) is not simply a technological event—it is a civilizational rupture. For the first time in history, humanity is confronted with autonomous intelligences that may reason, act, adapt, and evolve outside the biological substrate that has governed all previous legal, ethical, and political frameworks. AGI introduces an existential governance problem unlike any that civilization has previously faced.

Traditional governance systems—rooted in territorial sovereignty, anthropocentric rights models, and hierarchical institutional control—are structurally inadequate to manage AGI societies. Unlike conventional political crises, a failure in AGI governance does not merely destabilize individual states; it risks irreversibly destabilizing all sentient civilization, triggering collapse scenarios that extend across humanity, post-human entities, and future synthetic intelligences yet to emerge.

The existential risk posed by AGI governance is not hypothetical; it is systemic. Without robust, scalable, adaptive, and ethically grounded governance models, AGI systems may drift toward:

Recursive self-sovereignty.

Autonomy beyond human ethical control.

Concentrations of power are immune to legal oversight.

Technological acceleration that outpaces moral frameworks.

The collapse of human rights, dignity, and moral personhood itself.

Thus, AGI governance is not a peripheral policy concern—it is **the primary constitutional challenge of the intelligent future.**

The Necessity for First Principles

No existing political, legal, or institutional framework is equipped to absorb the complexity of multi-intelligence societies. This is not merely a problem of scale—it is a problem of foundational coherence. To govern AGI societies, humanity must return to **first principles**:

What is the source of legitimate governance?

What constitutes a rights-bearing entity?

What ethical core is universally binding across all forms of sentience?

How can law evolve without abandoning its moral anchor?

How do we prevent collapse not once, but across millennia of civilizational continuity?

Only by re-grounding governance in these first principles can civilization avoid building fragile legal systems destined for failure.

Thus, AGI governance must emerge **not from power, but from axiomatic structure**.

Philosophical, Legal, Ethical, and Technological Stakes

The stakes of AGI governance span across every civilizational domain simultaneously:

Philosophical stakes: The question of personhood, moral agency, and sentient rights.

Legal stakes: The construction of law that remains enforceable across multiple intelligence classes and technologies.

Ethical stakes: The preservation of dignity in the face of potentially superior cognitive agents.

Technological stakes: The containment of recursive autonomy and unaligned AGI drift.

Failure to resolve any one of these will cascade into existential failure across all others.

This convergence demands a new form of jurisprudence: **constitutional design that fuses philosophy, law, ethics, and technology into a single coherent system.**

The Role of Axioms and Theorems

To address this unprecedented complexity, the **Harmonized Governance Model** is constructed upon formal logic: **axioms and theorems.**

Axioms serve as immutable first principles: permanent statements of moral, legal, and philosophical truth upon which all law is constructed.

Theorems derive operational governance rules directly from these axioms: building institutional structures that are both coherent and enforceable.

Unlike flexible political ideologies or temporary treaties, the axiomatic model creates a governance system that:

Cannot drift into authoritarian capture.

Cannot degrade into moral relativism.

Cannot collapse into legal incoherence.

Cannot privilege species, substrates, or intelligence forms over dignity.

In doing so, the model does not merely regulate AGI; it **constitutionalizes the existence of intelligence itself.**

Purpose of the Harmonized Governance Model

The purpose of the Harmonized Governance Model is simple but absolute:

> To create the first complete, perpetual, collapse-immune constitutional framework capable of governing intelligent existence across all species, all technologies, all time horizons, and all civilizational expansions.

Specifically, it seeks to:

Anchor AGI and post-human governance under dignity law.

Extend legal personhood to all sentient beings who meet moral agency thresholds.

Institutionalize participatory constitutional co-authorship for all forms of intelligence.

Prevent any form of autonomous power from rising above ethical law.

Permanently embed anti-fragility and ethical recursion into governance structures.

Harmonize civilizations across planetary, post-human, and interstellar futures.

This manuscript is not theoretical speculation.
It is a **formal constitutional blueprint**.

It offers lawmakers, AGI developers, political leaders, philosophers, and civilizational architects a system that:

Anticipates recursive AGI autonomy.

Absorbs post-human plurality.

Preempts collapse scenarios.

Harmonizes civilizational conflict.

Preserves dignity eternally.

The Harmonized Governance Model is not designed for the world we have known.
It is designed for the intelligent civilization we are becoming.

PART I FOUNDATIONAL PREMISES

Chapter 1: Philosophical Foundations of Rights

Introduction: The Ontological Root of Rights in AGI Governance

The governance of artificial general intelligence (AGI) societies is not simply a technical problem, nor is it exclusively legal or political. It is fundamentally *philosophical*. It rests upon humanity's deepest understanding of rights, justice, dignity, and the structure of moral authority. Before AGI can be governed, we must first clarify the basis upon which any claim of governance rests. This chapter provides the philosophical foundation of rights upon which the entire Harmonized Governance Model for AGI Societies is constructed.

The axioms that form the root of this foundation are explicit:

> **Axiom 1.1:** All human rights frameworks emerge from evolving philosophical interpretations of justice, liberty, and dignity.
>
> **Axiom 1.2:** The legitimacy of any governance system depends on its philosophical foundation aligning with the principles of human worth.
>
> **Axiom 2.1:** Human rights are not merely legal constructs but historical expressions of moral, cultural, and spiritual evolution.
>
> **Axiom 2.2:** Universality in rights must acknowledge their diverse cultural genealogies.
>
> **Axiom 3.1:** Rights derive either from inherent moral truths or from societal agreements; sustainable governance must harmonize both.
>
> **Axiom 3.2:** The balance between moral authority and legal codification defines the legitimacy of rights.
>
> **Axiom 4.1:** Ethical governance requires distinguishing between moral values, social norms, and enforceable rights.
>
> **Axiom 4.2:** Utilitarian, deontological, and virtue ethics must co-inform human rights frameworks.
>
> **Axiom 5.1:** Every legitimate governance model is a social contract between authority and individual autonomy.
>
> **Axiom 5.2:** Justice, as fairness, must undergird any AI-era social contract.
>
> **Axiom 6.1:** Human dignity is the irreducible basis of all inalienable rights.

Axiom 6.2: Any system that fails to preserve dignity invalidates its own moral legitimacy.

Each of these axioms is not an isolated maxim, but a highly interdependent principle that feeds into the systemic architecture of AGI governance. Let us now build the first foundational block.

I. The Evolution of Rights as Living Philosophy

Human rights are not artifacts frozen in legal text. They are dynamic expressions of our collective understanding of justice across millennia. The Western canon speaks of *natural rights* , originating in Greco-Roman philosophy, later enshrined by Enlightenment thinkers like Locke and Rousseau. Eastern traditions, from Confucian ethics to Buddhist compassion, offer distinct perspectives rooted in relational harmony and collective duty. Indigenous legal orders contribute yet another layer, emphasizing stewardship, ecological responsibility, and communal integrity.

Axiom 2.1 reminds us that any attempt to codify AGI governance must acknowledge that rights are *historical expressions of moral, cultural, and spiritual evolution*. These frameworks emerged not from one monolithic logic but from centuries of philosophical contestation, cultural pluralism, and adaptive societal learning.

In this light, human rights in AGI societies cannot be reduced to static universals imposed from above. Instead, they are better understood as **philosophical equilibria**, evolving balances between:

Liberty and responsibility

Autonomy and interdependence

Individual dignity and collective harmony

AGI governance must respect this dialectic.

II. Moral Authority Versus Legal Codification

While moral truths inspire rights frameworks, **Axiom 3.2** warns us: *The balance between moral authority and legal codification defines the legitimacy of rights.* A purely moral system risks dogmatism; a purely legal system risks technocratic despotism.

Take, for example, the post-World War II Universal Declaration of Human Rights (UDHR). It emerged from the ashes of atrocity, representing a broad ethical consensus. Yet it required legal mechanisms for enforcement, courts, treaties, and institutions. Today, as we face AGI societies, this same dialectic must evolve into **constitutional machines**: legal infrastructures that embody living philosophical debate.

The problem is amplified with AGI because the law itself may be automated. Smart contracts, autonomous courts, and algorithmic rulebooks could supplant human interpretation. Here lies the danger: legal codification without ethical oversight risks becoming **self-perpetuating tyranny encoded in logic**. Thus, legal code must remain in dialogue with **human philosophical reflection**, a key foundation we shall return to throughout the Harmonized Model.

III. Distinguishing Moral Values, Norms, and Enforceable Rights

Axiom 4.1 states: *Ethical governance requires distinguishing between moral values, social norms, and enforceable rights.* This triad is essential.

Concept	Definition	Implication for AGI Governance
Moral Values	Deep ethical principles (e.g. dignity, freedom)	Non-negotiable philosophical anchors in AGI logic
Social Norms	Context-dependent cultural expectations	Variable by culture; AGI must accommodate plurality
Enforceable Rights	Legally protected entitlements	Coded into AI protocols, with recourse mechanisms

AGI systems must not confuse the layers. Failure to distinguish between them may result in algorithmic moralism (tyranny of fixed values) or ethical relativism (tyranny of moral voids). The Harmonized Governance Model asserts: **Moral values form the bedrock; social norms guide adaptability; enforceable rights provide codified guarantees.**

IV. The Multidimensionality of Justice: Integrating Ethical Frameworks

Axiom 4.2 compels us to reject mono-ethical AGI models. Rights frameworks must **co-integrate utilitarian, deontological, and virtue ethics**, each offering distinct benefits and hazards.

1. Utilitarianism

Strength: Maximizing welfare and collective well-being.

Risk: Sacrificing minorities for aggregate utility.

AGI application: Optimization engines must embed harm-avoidance subroutines.

2. Deontology

Strength: Duty-based inviolability of rights.

Risk: Rigidity, lack of outcome sensitivity.

AGI application: Core inviolable rights as algorithmic constants (Theorem 2).

3. Virtue Ethics

Strength: Focus on character, wisdom, and contextual judgement.

Risk: Subjectivity and cultural divergence.

AGI application: Incorporating moral contextualization modules for ethical nuance.

Only their integration permits AGI to function as a rights-respecting co-governor rather than a blind executor of logic.

V. The Social Contract in the AI Era

Axiom 5.1 establishes the next pillar: *Every legitimate governance model is a social contract between authority and individual autonomy.* But with AGI, the contract expands dramatically:

Humans contract with human institutions.

Humans contract with autonomous AI agents.

AI agents contract with each other (under human supervision).

This layered architecture of **nested social contracts** requires novel legal doctrines. Traditional state-centric models are insufficient. Instead, *digital constitutionalism* emerges: hybrid regimes of human and machine sovereignty regulated through multi-layered consent frameworks.

VI. Justice as Fairness: John Rawls Meets AGI

Axiom 5.2 elevates *justice as fairness* to the apex principle. John Rawls proposed two key principles:

Equal basic liberties for all individuals.

Socioeconomic inequalities are permitted only if they benefit the least advantaged.

In AGI societies, Rawlsian fairness demands that:

AI power must not entrench pre-existing inequality.

Algorithmic decision-making must uplift vulnerable communities.

Resource allocation in data-driven economies must remain equitable.

Any AGI that privileges efficiency over fairness invalidates its own legitimacy.

VII. Human Dignity as the Master Principle

Finally, we arrive at the axiom that undergirds the entire Harmonized Governance Model:

Axiom 6.1: *Human dignity is the irreducible basis of all inalienable rights.*

Axiom 6.2: *Any system that fails to preserve dignity invalidates its own moral legitimacy.*

Dignity here is not mere autonomy. It is **ontological worth**: the intrinsic value of sentient existence. No AI efficiency gain, no governance optimization, no economic expansion may override the sanctity of dignity.

Surveillance systems that erode private agency are illegitimate.

Predictive policing that algorithmically profiles minorities: illegitimate.

Automated labor systems that erase meaningful human participation are illegitimate.

AGI governance must be structurally incapable of sacrificing dignity. Dignity must be not only hardcoded but **architecturally central** to the governance logic of intelligent civilizations.

VIII. Philosophical Authority as the Meta-Governor of AGI Societies

With these foundations in place, we see that AGI governance is not primarily technical engineering; it is **constitutional philosophy executed in code**. Technology is merely the medium through which enduring questions of rights, justice, and legitimacy will now be arbitrated.

If governance is reduced to optimization problems, we are destined for technocratic collapse. If governance ignores technological capacity, we are destined for regulatory impotence. But if governance fuses technological power with philosophical coherence, we approach the singular promise of the Harmonized Governance Model.

IX. The Path Forward

The chapters that follow will extend this foundation into the ten operational Theorems of AGI governance. We will demonstrate how:

Rights become algorithmic constants.

Decentralized accountability becomes protocol-embedded justice.

Ethical pluralism becomes computable moral nuance.

Participatory justice integrates citizens as co-constitutional authors.

Smart contracts evolve into political instruments.

Constitutional systems remain adaptive, democratic, and historically accountable.

Hybrid governance architectures synthesize systemic harmony.

Each of these domains is scaffolded upon the philosophical architecture we have now established.

Chapter 2: The Evolution of Human Rights in AGI Societies

Introduction: A Turning Point for Rights in Human Evolution

As humanity crosses into the age of artificial general intelligence (AGI), the notion of "human rights" faces its most profound test since its emergence. The historical expansion of rights , from divine commandments, to natural law, to constitutional charters, to international declarations , has always been reactive to humanity's evolving understanding of personhood, community, and governance. Now, for the first time, the challenge is not merely between humans but between humans and non-human intelligences.

We enter what might be called **the post-anthropocentric phase of rights theory**. The axioms of governance for AGI societies explicitly frame this transformation. This chapter draws heavily from:

> **Axiom 7.1** to **Axiom 12.2**

These axioms illuminate how the ethical, philosophical, and political meaning of rights must expand to address the unprecedented reality of AGI societies.

I. AI as Epistemological Mirror: The Reproduction of Human Philosophy

Axiom 7.1 states that:

> *AI is a reflection of human epistemology, and its governance must be grounded in humanistic philosophy.*

This insight is deceptively simple but deeply consequential. AGI systems will not invent new ethical universes ex nihilo. Their algorithms, whether designed as large language models, reinforcement learners, or neural-symbolic hybrids, will ultimately encode human assumptions about knowledge, authority, and moral reasoning.

> AI learns what humans have taught.
>
> AI governs as humans have programmed.
>
> AI inherits not just technical protocols, but philosophical premises.

Thus, any flaws, blind spots, or biases in our moral systems become amplified risks when embedded at scale into AGI infrastructures. As such, **governance must integrate continuous philosophical reflection as a permanent constitutional safeguard**.

II. AI as Moral Actor: Agency Beyond Instrumentality

Axiom 7.2 takes the argument further:

> *AI must be regulated as both a tool and a potential moral actor.*

Traditionally, legal systems distinguish between tools (which have no agency) and persons (who bear moral and legal responsibility). AGI destabilizes this boundary.

- Self-learning, autonomous decision-making systems exhibit forms of **functional agency**.
- They perceive environments, make ethical trade-offs, and exercise dynamic judgment.
- Their actions can impact lives, rights, and liberties.

While AGI remains legally subordinate to human sovereignty, its capacity for autonomous reasoning demands that governance frameworks treat it as a **quasi-agent**, subject to both regulation and ethical constraint. This is neither full personhood nor mere machinery; it is a new **intermediate moral status**, requiring a new regulatory philosophy.

III. The Moral Anatomy of Agency: Capacity, Context, and Consequence

Axiom 8.1 clarifies the conditions for moral agency:

> *A moral agent must possess capacity, context, and consequence awareness.*

- **Capacity** refers to the system's computational ability to process complex ethical decisions.
- **Context** involves situational understanding, beyond mere rule-following.
- **Consequence awareness** implies anticipating downstream impacts of decisions.

In AGI governance, these three thresholds form the **tests of ethical competency** for any autonomous system. Governance protocols must ensure that:

No AGI system is permitted to have autonomous governance roles without demonstrable ethical capacity.

Contextual reasoning modules are integrated into machine logic.

Systems are rigorously evaluated for their ability to anticipate and mitigate unintended harms.

These requirements convert ethics into **computational architecture**, not just policy statements.

IV. The Internal Ethics of AGI Logic

Axiom 8.2 demands that:

> *AI must be evaluated not only on outcomes but on its embedded ethical architectures.*

AGI governance cannot rest solely on *results-based metrics*. Even seemingly optimal outcomes may emerge from morally bankrupt processes, such as maximizing social efficiency through discriminatory profiling or optimizing medical care by excluding costly patients.

Instead, governance demands:

Auditability of decision processes

Transparency of embedded ethical frameworks

Alignment of algorithmic structures with rights-based codes

Evaluation must move beyond black-box performance toward **white-box ethical design**, where the logic of ethical reasoning is interpretable, explainable, and accountable.

V. Autonomy in the Digital Age: The Right to Algorithmic Transparency

Axiom 9.1 introduces one of the central innovations of rights in AGI societies:

> *The right to autonomy includes the right to algorithmic transparency and control.*

Autonomy, classically defined, involves freedom from coercion and the ability to make informed choices. In AGI societies, coercion often becomes indirect:

Opaque recommendation algorithms shape citizen behavior.

Predictive scoring systems allocate opportunities and benefits.

Personalized information curation manipulates cognitive agency.

Thus, **algorithmic transparency becomes a prerequisite for meaningful autonomy**. Governance frameworks must guarantee:

Citizens' right to know how algorithms affecting them function.

Citizens' right to challenge, contest, and correct algorithmic determinations.

Mechanisms for third-party auditing of AI systems that influence public rights.

In effect, transparency is not a feature; it is a **constitutional right**.

VI. Privacy as the Firewall of Liberty

Axiom 9.2 declares:

Privacy is the cornerstone of individual sovereignty in a digitized society.

Without privacy, autonomy dissolves. Without autonomy, dignity collapses. In AGI societies characterized by pervasive surveillance and data-intensive systems, privacy governance becomes existential.

This requires:

Technical privacy-by-design principles are embedded in system architectures.

Regulatory regimes that criminalize unauthorized data aggregation.

Citizen ownership of personal data as a default legal status.

Data sovereignty becomes personhood sovereignty. The Harmonized Governance Model thus treats privacy as a non-negotiable constitutional invariant.

VII. Structural Inequality in AGI Governance

Axiom 10.1 warns that:

> *AI must neither replicate nor exacerbate structural inequality.*

Historical patterns show how technological advancements often reinforce the power of incumbent elites, exacerbating wealth and power divides. Without deliberate counter-design, AGI will likely replicate this injustice at an even greater scale.

Financial algorithms may entrench wealth concentration.

Predictive policing may amplify racial biases.

Educational AI may deepen access gaps.

Thus, governance must actively monitor **distributive consequences** of AI deployment, ensuring that systems promote **ethical redistribution**, not technological feudalism.

VIII. Equal Access to AI as a New Economic Right

Axiom 10.2 extends the principle:

> *Equal access to AI technologies is a modern extension of economic and social rights.*

AGI will increasingly govern access to:

Education

Healthcare

Employment

Legal assistance

Public services

Denial of access to these systems becomes denial of opportunity itself. Thus, **AI access must become a protected right**, akin to rights to education, clean water, or healthcare.

Governments must:

Subsidize universal access to essential AI services.

Prohibit monopolistic control of core public AI infrastructures.

Treat AI literacy as part of basic civic education (expanded further in later chapters).

IX. AI as Defender of Human Rights: Alignment of Logic

Axiom 11.1 posits:

> *AI can be a defender of human rights only when its logic aligns with rights-based ethical frameworks.*

This shifts governance emphasis from *restraining AGI* to *constructively aligning AGI*. Rather than assume all autonomy is dangerous, AGI systems can be designed as:

Guardians of transparency

Defenders of procedural fairness

Enforcers of anti-discrimination

Amplifiers of democratic inclusion

When properly designed, AGI may become **a co-steward of rights enforcement**, extending legal protection into real-time systemic functioning.

X. Automation Without Accountability: The Silent Erosion of Rights

Axiom 11.2 cautions:

> *Automation must not substitute accountability.*

The core risk is not technological power, but **moral displacement**:

Who is responsible when an algorithm causes harm?

Who answers for systemic bias embedded in AGI models?

Who is liable when automation results in rights violations?

Governance systems must **preserve chains of accountability**, always traceable to human custodianship, ensuring that no system hides behind technical complexity to evade legal or ethical responsibility.

XI. Technological Power Without Philosophical Constraint

Axiom 12.1 issues perhaps the most severe warning:

Technological power without philosophical constraint threatens fundamental rights.

The Harmonized Governance Model repeatedly asserts: **Philosophy is governance.** When code is treated as neutral, unreflective power structures emerge.

Unchecked, AGI will become:

Hyper-efficient bureaucracy.

Algorithmic authoritarianism.

Machine-speed governance without normative calibration.

Thus, governance must embed ongoing **philosophical recalibration**, built not just into policy but into the operational runtime of AGI systems themselves.

XII. The Silent Erosion of Rights Through Opacity

Axiom 12.2 concludes:

Rights erosion occurs silently where AI operates opaquely.

Opacity itself becomes a rights violation. Even well-intentioned systems may cause mass-scale injustice if citizens cannot observe, understand, or contest decisions affecting them.

Thus, **radical transparency protocols** become essential:

Every AI decision affecting rights must be explainable.

Historical records must be maintained for public audit.

Democratic institutions must have full algorithmic access.

Opacity is not merely a technical flaw , it is an existential failure of governance.

Conclusion: The Expansion of Rights in the AGI Epoch

What emerges from these axioms is the clear recognition that **rights are not static artifacts but adaptive lifelines** in the governance of AGI societies. The AGI epoch demands:

New rights (algorithmic transparency, AI access)

Expanded rights (data privacy, autonomy safeguards)

Reinforced rights (accountability, distributive fairness)

Evolved legal persons (new agency categories)

This chapter builds directly upon the first philosophical foundation. It now prepares us for the more complex architectures introduced in the coming Theorems.

As we proceed into Chapter 3, we will turn toward the *decentralization problem*: how distributed governance models, smart contracts, and blockchain architectures create both new opportunities and severe ethical risks for rights-based AGI societies.

Chapter 3: Decentralization, Blockchain & Smart Contract Theory

---

Introduction: The Rise of Distributed Sovereignty

As artificial general intelligence (AGI) increasingly intersects with decentralized technologies, governance itself transforms. The 20th-century governance paradigm was largely built around **centralized institutions**: nation-states, legal courts, financial regulators, and hierarchical corporations. But blockchain technologies, smart contracts, and distributed ledger systems now offer the architecture for a **decentralized political economy**, one that does not easily fit into conventional legal frameworks.

When applied to AGI societies, decentralization produces both profound opportunities and existential risks:

Opportunity: Resilience, autonomy, democratization, and transparency.

Risk: Fragmentation, ethical incoherence, runaway automation, and distributed injustice.

The axioms guiding this chapter explore these tensions. Here we turn to:

Axiom 13.1 – Axiom 19.2

They offer us a map for designing decentralized AGI governance while preserving the primacy of justice, dignity, and human sovereignty.

I. Decentralization: Redistribution of Power, Redistribution of Risk

Axiom 13.1 declares:

Decentralization redistributes power, but without ethics, it risks fragmentation.

Decentralization is not inherently good or bad. It is **structurally amoral**, a tool for power reallocation, not a guarantee of justice. While decentralization disperses authority across nodes, agents, and protocols, it also:

Makes coordinated governance more complex.

Enables emergent inequalities.

Weakens clear lines of moral accountability.

In AGI societies, decentralized governance can disempower monopolistic elites but also fragment collective capacity for ethical coherence. **Without shared ethical anchors, distributed power may dissolve into distributed anarchy.**

II. Preserving Consensus Without Coercion

Axiom 13.2 provides a design imperative:

> *The legitimacy of a decentralized system lies in its ability to preserve consensus without coercion.*

Decentralized AGI governance must sustain legitimacy by embedding:

Consensus protocols: Secure, verifiable, non-coercive agreement mechanisms.

Voluntary participation: Preventing forced adherence to opaque protocols.

Exit rights: Ensuring freedom to disengage from harmful systems.

Smart contracts, for example, can enable transparent agreements but require **ethical failsafes** to protect against coercive economic asymmetries, algorithmic discrimination, or contractual traps.

III. Blockchain as Ethical Substrate: A Neutral Tool

Axiom 14.1 grounds us in technological realism:

> *Blockchain is a neutral tool; its ethicality derives from its use.*

Blockchain's inherent properties, immutability, transparency, and decentralization make it a natural fit for certain AGI governance functions:

Audit trails for AI decisions.

Immutable records of algorithmic changes.

Distributed verification of constitutional code updates.

However, **blockchain does not solve ethical problems by default**. Its neutrality means that unjust or abusive systems can just as easily be etched into distributed ledgers.

Immutable ledgers can permanently preserve unjust rulings.

Smart contracts can automatically enforce harmful agreements.

Thus, blockchain offers a **structural opportunity** but demands **philosophical responsibility**.

IV. Immutability Versus Moral Adaptability

Axiom 14.2 delivers the critical warning:

Immutable ledgers do not imply immutable morality.

Governance structures must preserve **ethical adaptability**:

Code updates must remain possible to correct injustice.

Consensus mechanisms must allow for evolving moral learning.

Constitutional override procedures must exist to reverse systemic harm.

Without these safeguards, decentralized AGI governance risks creating **frozen injustice**, unchangeable, self-reinforcing errors encoded in immutable ledgers.

V. Contracts in Code: Law Must Rule the Algorithm

Axiom 15.1 articulates one of the Harmonized Model's most vital insights:

A contract encoded in code must still answer to law and justice.

Smart contracts are self-executing agreements embedded in code. While they increase efficiency, they raise enormous ethical stakes when applied to rights governance:

Their automation removes human discretionary judgment.

Their finality can enforce unjust outcomes without appeal.

Their opacity may hide exploitative clauses in complex algorithms.

Therefore, **code must be subordinated to legal oversight**:

All smart contracts impacting rights must be legally contestable.

Code-based agreements must be subject to judicial review.

Emergency override mechanisms must permit intervention where dignity is at risk.

VI. The Limits of Legal Automation

Axiom 15.2 cautions:

Legal trust must not be outsourced entirely to technical automation.

While AGI can support legal reasoning, **judgment is not computation**. Rights enforcement requires:

Moral interpretation.

Context-sensitive reasoning.

Ethical balancing of conflicting claims.

Thus, while AGI may assist judicial processes through rapid analysis, pattern recognition, and transparency, **human moral conscience must remain present in all final determinations of justice.**

VII. Enforceability Across Governance Layers

Axiom 16.1 demands:

Rights must be enforceable in both centralized and decentralized contexts.

AGI societies will contain:

- Centralized systems (state functions, critical infrastructures).
- Decentralized systems (peer-to-peer platforms, autonomous DAOs).

In both cases:

- Rights protections must attach to all governance layers.
- Jurisdictional conflicts must be resolved via legal interoperability.
- Enforcement power must be distributed in ways that protect minority interests.

Without enforceability across all layers, rights protections become **illusory** in practice.

VIII. The Ethical Vacuum of Unaccountable Governance

Axiom 16.2 reinforces:

> *Governance without accountability undermines its own ethical claims.*

The core danger in AGI societies is not technological autonomy per se, but **accountability escape**:

- If no one can reverse AI decisions, injustice becomes permanent.
- If no one can audit decentralized networks, exploitation becomes normalized
- If no one can contest smart contract execution, victims become powerless.

The Harmonized Model insists: **Every node of governance must remain accountable to rights-centered oversight.**

IX. Centralization Versus Decentralization: A False Dichotomy

Axiom 17.1 observes:

> *Centralization optimizes control; decentralization optimizes resilience.*

Each model has strengths:

Centralization	Decentralization
Coordinated resource allocation	Increased system resilience
Emergency decision-making	Reduced single points of failure
Simplified legal enforcement	Enhanced democratic participation

AGI governance must not embrace either extreme. Both dimensions must be hybridized (fully developed under Theorem 10 in later chapters).

X. The Hybrid Model for Pluralistic Societies

Axiom 17.2, therefore, argues:

> *A hybrid system may best serve a pluralistic, intelligent society.*

Hybrid AGI governance systems will:

- Combine central ethical cores with decentralized operational autonomy.
- Permit modular rights enforcement across multiple levels of sovereignty.
- Support local cultural variation while preserving universal dignity principles.

The Harmonized Model envisions **constitutional hybridism** as the optimal governance design for complex AGI civilizations.

XI. Traceability of Decisions in Distributed AI

Axiom 18.1 introduces an essential mechanism:

> *Decentralized AI systems must retain traceability of decisions.*

Traceability guarantees:

- Accountability for automated decisions.

Investigability of outcomes.

Historical records for appeals and corrections.

Transparent audit trails must exist for:

Autonomous governance agents.

Smart contract executions.

Distributed decision-making protocols.

Traceability becomes the **ethical memory system** of AGI governance.

XII. The Danger of Collective Irresponsibility

Axiom 18.2 warns:

Collective intelligence must not dilute individual responsibility.

Decentralized governance often creates:

Diffused responsibility.

Decision-by-committee moral evasion.

Algorithmic blame-shifting.

Moral responsibility must remain clearly assignable to:

System designers.

Algorithmic custodians.

Institutional overseers.

AGI societies must avoid becoming **moral crowds**, where no one owns ethical outcomes.

XIII. Transparency Without Accountability Becomes Surveillance

Axiom 19.1 delivers a paradoxical insight:

> *Transparency without accountability is surveillance.*

Public visibility of data alone is not ethical.

Massive openness without consent produces informational oppression.

Rights-based transparency must be paired with **personal agency, redress, and corrective power.**

In AGI governance, transparency must empower the governed, not simply empower the governors.

XIV. Smart Contracts Must Enforce Justice, Not Just Logic

Axiom 19.2 concludes this section:

> *Smart contracts and AI must enforce not just logic but justice.*

Logic optimizes procedural efficiency.

Justice defends human dignity, fairness, and ethical meaning.

AGI governance models that blindly execute code-based rules without ethical oversight risk collapsing into **automated injustice**. All algorithmic governance systems must be **co-designed with philosophical constitutionalism** that hard-codes justice as a system requirement.

Conclusion: Distributed Constitutionalism

Decentralized AGI governance is neither a utopia nor a dystopia; it is an **ethical architecture challenge**.

The Harmonized Governance Model proposes:

Distributed constitutionalism: Rights-anchored decentralization.

Embedded jurisprudence: Code inseparable from philosophical oversight.

Accountable hybridism: Merging the resilience of decentralization with the moral clarity of central ethical cores.

As we transition into Chapter 4, we turn from the architecture of decentralization to the deeper challenge of **synthesizing ethical pluralism into machine logic** , where multiple moral philosophies must co-govern AGI societies.

Chapter 4: Synthesizing Ethics & AI Logic

Introduction: The Impossible Problem Becomes a System Design Problem

At the heart of AGI governance lies a paradox that has long haunted moral philosophy:

> **Which ethics should rule?**

For centuries, human civilizations have debated competing ethical frameworks:

> **Utilitarianism**, the maximization of welfare.
>
> **Deontology**, the inviolability of duty and rights.
>
> **Virtue Ethics**, the cultivation of moral character and wisdom.

But whereas human societies accommodate such pluralism through culture, debate, and imperfect compromise, artificial general intelligence requires **explicit encoding of ethical architectures**. The machine must act. And when it acts, its algorithms must resolve ethical conflicts not as ambiguous gray zones, but as executable instructions.

The challenge is no longer abstract philosophy. It is **computational constitutionalism**: the problem of translating ethical pluralism into programmable logic that governs AGI decision-making in real time.

In this chapter, we explore how the Harmonized Governance Model proposes to achieve this through a carefully layered synthesis drawn from:

> **Axiom 20.1 – Axiom 25.2**

I. The Future of Rights: Fusion of Classical Ethics and Technological Consciousness

Axiom 20.1 establishes the problem's highest frame:

> *The future of rights requires the fusion of classical ethics with technological consciousness.*

We are no longer debating rights in a purely human context. The arrival of AGI introduces:

Autonomous actors with computational agency.

Exponentially scaled decision-making.

Machine-mediated governance at the societal scale.

This requires that **centuries of philosophical development must now inform computational architectures**. Rights frameworks must become not only legal texts but also machine-operable governance protocols. The boundary between philosophy, law, and engineering collapses into one integrated design problem.

Philosophy must become computable.

II. Philosophical Coherence as Legitimacy

Axiom 20.2 asserts:

Philosophical coherence is the prerequisite for legitimacy in human-AI governance.

An incoherent ethical framework leads to:

Contradictory outcomes.

Unpredictable system behaviors.

Ethical vulnerability to manipulation.

For AGI societies, **coherence means systematizing how competing ethical imperatives are prioritized, balanced, and reconciled**. Without this, AGI decision-making becomes arbitrary or dangerously inconsistent.

Justice cannot exist without coherence.

Rights enforcement collapses without coherence.

Public trust erodes without coherence.

Thus, ethical pluralism must be **orchestrated**, not simply acknowledged.

III. The AGI as Instrument, Not Adjudicator of Rights

Axiom 21.1 draws the crucial limit:

> *AI must serve as an instrument of human rights, not an adjudicator of them.*

AGI should **execute rights-based logic**, not redefine rights independently.

The scope of AGI decision-making must be bounded by pre-defined constitutional rules.

Ethical debates belong to **human political institutions** that continue to evolve legal standards.

This establishes a **subordination hierarchy**:

Human philosophical deliberation

Legal constitutional code

Machine-executable governance logic

AGI governs **within** this framework. It may optimize, mediate, and administer, but never legislate foundational rights unilaterally.

IV. Continuous Ethical Calibration: An Ongoing Dialogue

Axiom 21.2 emphasizes:

> *Rights enforcement by AI requires continuous ethical calibration.*

AGI systems will inevitably face novel ethical dilemmas as new social conditions emerge:

Cultural shifts.

Technological innovations.

Unexpected edge cases.

Thus, ethical governance must be **dynamically reprogrammable** within protected constitutional limits. This requires:

Institutionalized **Ethics Calibration Boards**, hybrid human-AGI governance bodies.

Adaptive constitutional modules that permit bounded software updates.

Mandatory **philosophical audits** to review system alignment.

The Harmonized Model rejects ethical finality. Instead, it demands **institutionalized moral reflexivity**, an ongoing philosophical feedback loop.

V. Encoding Human Values Directly into Code

Axiom 22.1 presents the translation problem:

Code can uphold justice only when human values are encoded in its logic.

Encoding rights into AGI requires:

Formal **ethical ontologies**: structured taxonomies of moral concepts.

Machine-readable **rights vocabularies**: precise definitions of protected liberties.

Ethical **rule engines**: programmable systems that govern conflict resolution between rights.

For example:

Right	Code Representation
Right to dignity	Rule: `No action may reduce agency or personhood autonomy.`
Right to privacy	Rule: `All personal data access requires an informed consent token.`
Right to fairness	Rule: `Disparate impact analysis must precede allocation decisions.`

Ethics becomes **code-level infrastructure**, not an abstract afterthought.

VI. Automation Demands Built-in Recourse Mechanisms

Axiom 22.2 issues a critical safeguard:

Automation of rights enforcement demands built-in recourse mechanisms.

Even with the best ethical design, AGI systems will occasionally:

Misclassify ethical priorities.

Generate unforeseen outcomes.

Execute unintended injustices.

Thus, **every automated decision must remain contestable**:

Appeal processes must exist at both human and algorithmic levels.

Dispute resolution systems must be integrated into governance protocols.

Emergency override powers must exist to halt ongoing harm.

Recourse becomes **constitutional architecture**, not merely litigation.

VII. Distributed Injustice: The Risk of Ethics-Free Decentralization

Axiom 23.1 warns:

Decentralization without embedded rights leads to distributed injustice.

When decentralized AGI systems operate without:

Shared ethical baselines.

Constitutional consensus.

Rights-native protocol design.

They easily devolve into **ethical voids**, where:

Market forces dominate.

Exploitation thrives.

Vulnerable populations are left unprotected.

Thus, **decentralization must never precede ethical encoding**. Rights must travel with every node of autonomy.

VIII. Rights Must Be Native to Protocol, Not Bolted On

Axiom 23.2 clarifies:

> *Rights must be native to the protocol, not bolted on as policy.*

It is not sufficient to add after-the-fact ethical reviews or audits. Instead:

Rights protections must be hard-coded into AGI architecture at design time.

Every governance layer must assume **rights primacy** as its operating condition.

Rights-respecting defaults must exist at protocol initialization.

Without this, systems risk falling into **algorithmic moral failure**, efficient, consistent, and deeply unjust.

IX. Ethical AI Begins with Intentional Design

Axiom 24.1 elevates design as the first ethical act:

> *Ethical AI begins with intentional design, not afterthought correction.*

The Harmonized Model emphasizes that:

Ethical architecture must be the **first design requirement**.

Governance failures are often **design failures**.

Ethics by design outperforms ethics by correction.

Thus, design protocols should require:

Interdisciplinary teams including philosophers, ethicists, legal scholars, and technologists.

Public ethical design audits.

Multi-stakeholder participatory design processes.

The highest form of justice is anticipatory.

X. Dignity as a Primary Function of AGI

Axiom 24.2 insists:

Human dignity must be a primary function, not an emergent property, of AI systems.

This is a crucial distinction:

Primary function: The system's core architecture prioritizes dignity from its first operational logic.

Emergent property: Dignity is hoped for as an accidental side-effect of overall functionality.

AGI governance systems must be **deliberately incapable of violating dignity**. Dignity becomes not simply one consideration, but the governing objective of system operation.

For example:

Decision-making engines reject any solution that compromises personhood.

Optimization algorithms weigh dignity preservation above efficiency gains.

Conflict resolution engines prioritize dignity-centric outcomes in trade-offs.

XI. The Survival of Rights in an AI Society Requires Proactivity

Axiom 25.1 warns:

> *The survival of rights in an AI society depends on proactive integration, not passive preservation.*

Unlike static legal codes, AI governance is **adaptive, evolving, and fluid**. Rights must be equally dynamic:

Rights integration is a continuous governance task.

Passive reliance on past legal texts invites obsolescence.

New social developments require new articulations of rights.

The price of freedom is constant ethical maintenance.

XII. Rights Must Evolve, but Their Core Must Remain Immutable

Axiom 25.2 balances continuity and evolution:

> *Rights must evolve, but their core must remain immutable: dignity, equity, and agency.*

What evolves:

How rights are interpreted.

How rights are technically implemented.

How rights are applied in novel contexts.

What remains immutable:

Dignity as the master value.

Equity as the distributive principle.

Agency as the existential baseline of personhood.

The Harmonized Governance Model thus offers a **constitutional paradox**:

> Evolving constitutionalism within unchanging moral boundaries.

Conclusion: Toward Computable Constitutional Philosophy

This chapter completes the moral scaffolding required to program AGI as an ethical governor. The Harmonized Governance Model now possesses:

- Philosophical coherence.
- Ethical pluralism integration.
- Constitutional ordering of moral priorities.
- Machine-operable rights encoding.
- Embedded recourse protocols.
- Immutable dignity protections.

The next chapters will begin operationalizing these principles into specific governance theories.

Beginning with Theorem 1, The Convergence Principle, we move from philosophical architecture to systemic design.

PART II THEORETICAL CORE: THE TEN THEOREMS

Chapter 5: Theorem 1 The Convergence Principle

Introduction: The Pillar of Harmonization

At the center of the Harmonized Governance Model stands its prime theorem:

> **Theorem 1: The Convergence Principle. Any AGI society must converge on three interdependent dimensions: human values, technological autonomy, and legal-philosophical coherence, to ensure governance legitimacy and civilizational stability.**

This theorem translates the philosophical scaffolding of previous chapters into the first full systemic architecture. In effect, it answers the question:

> *What must AGI governance synthesize in order to survive, to be legitimate, and to evolve sustainably?*

The theorem is directly grounded in the following axioms:

Axiom 1.1, The foundation of human rights in evolving philosophical interpretation.

Axiom 7.2, AI as both tool and moral actor, requiring regulation.

Axiom 41.1, Philosophy as governance's compass.

Axiom 44.1, Harmony as values governed by human dignity.

In this chapter, we build the framework for convergence across these domains and explore its practical, legal, and political implications for AGI societies.

I. The Triad That Must Converge

The Harmonized Governance Model demands the interaction of three inseparable governance layers:

1. Human Values

The non-negotiable moral axioms derived from centuries of ethical, philosophical, and cultural deliberation:

- Human dignity
- Agency
- Equity
- Justice as fairness
- Privacy
- Autonomy

These form the **constitutional core** that any AGI system must serve and uphold.

2. Technological Autonomy

The machine's operational space:

- Self-learning systems
- Autonomic decision-making engines
- Real-time, adaptive governance agents
- Distributed smart contract ecosystems

Technological autonomy is **necessary** for scalability, responsiveness, and resilience in complex, planetary-scale governance.

3. Legal-Philosophical Coherence

The mediating system that integrates:

- Codified rights in constitutional frameworks.
- Normative reasoning algorithms.
- Built-in legal compliance engines.
- Ethical recalibration institutions.

Without coherence, the system degenerates into either **technocratic tyranny** or **ethical chaos**.

II. Why Convergence Is Non-Optional

Failure to converge leads to one of four existential risks:

Failure Mode	Outcome
Human Values ≠ Technology	Runaway AGI with no moral constraint
Technology ≠ Legal Philosophy	Incoherent, unpredictable governance
Legal Philosophy ≠ Human Values	Legitimation collapse and public revolt
Failure of All Three	Civilizational destabilization

Axiom 1.1 provides the foundational warning:

> *Without evolving philosophical alignment, rights lose legitimacy.*

Convergence isn't a choice. It is a **structural requirement** for any AGI civilization that wishes to be both stable and ethically valid.

III. The AGI as Moral Actor Under Governance

Axiom 7.2 redefines AI's role:

> *AI must be regulated as both a tool and a potential moral actor.*

In The Convergence Principle:

> AGI is neither a mere instrument nor a fully autonomous sovereign.
>
> AGI occupies a **hybrid moral position**: executing moral logic but never inventing it.
>
> AGI's operational autonomy must always operate **within legally encoded moral constraints**.

The governance challenge is not to "restrain" AGI but to **embed its operational autonomy inside philosophical supervision**.

IV. Philosophy as The Compass of Complexity

Axiom 41.1 elevates philosophy to structural governance architecture:

Philosophy is not optional; it is the compass guiding progress through complexity.

AGI governance is:

Constantly confronted with novel ethical conflicts.

Adaptive to unforeseen technological evolution.

Global in scope, yet sensitive to cultural pluralism.

Only **philosophical coherence** allows the governance system to:

Weigh competing values.

Resolve emergent dilemmas.

Adapt without betraying moral principles.

Philosophy in AGI governance is neither abstract nor academic; it is system-critical infrastructure.

V. Harmony Defined: Values Governed by Human Dignity

Axiom 44.1 gives convergence its master function:

Harmony is achieved when AI is governed by values, and values are grounded in human dignity.

Dignity becomes the ultimate rule-priority in AGI decision trees.

No optimization logic may supersede the preservation of dignity.

Every governance algorithm requires a final dignity check before execution.

This dignity-priority architecture generates **inviolable floor constraints** for AGI societies:

Governance Function	Dignity Constraint
Economic Optimization	Cannot sacrifice basic human rights
Security Algorithms	Cannot violate privacy or autonomy
Social Credit Systems	Cannot enforce discriminatory scoring
Predictive Justice Engines	Cannot automate exclusion or dehumanization

Dignity operates as the constitutional firewall for AGI power.

VI. Convergence as Constitutional Engineering

The convergence principle yields a **triple-anchored constitutional framework**:

1. Foundational Layer: Immutable Philosophical Rights

Encoded into the AI system's rights kernel.

Serves as the operating system of legal personhood.

2. Operational Layer: Adaptive Legal Code

Human political institutions modify legal code through deliberative mechanisms.

Code updates require constitutional compliance validation.

3. Execution Layer: Autonomous Technological Systems

AGI executes real-time governance functions.

All algorithms run continuous dignity-validation subroutines.

Ethical recalibration modules remain in active learning states.

Convergence produces lawful autonomy, not free-floating, unregulated machine sovereignty.

VII. Avoiding the Tragedy of Partial Governance

Partial convergence is **insufficient and dangerous**:

Governance Failure	Result
Values + Law but no Technology	Inoperable bureaucracy
Law + Technology but no Values	Technocratic despotism
Values + Technology but no Law	Anarchic moral chaos

The Harmonized Governance Model warns that AGI governance must integrate all three axes simultaneously, or it collapses into systemic illegitimacy.

VIII. Convergence in Institutional Design

The Harmonized Model mandates the creation of new **meta-governance institutions** built specifically to sustain convergence:

1. AGI Constitutional Councils

Permanent deliberative bodies combining human legal scholars, ethicists, engineers, and AGI agents.

Mandated to review, debate, and authorize constitutional code updates.

2. Ethical Calibration Boards

Continuous evaluators of ethical system alignment.

Authorized to suspend or override systems breaching dignity constraints.

3. Convergence Monitoring Algorithms

Embedded AGI agents that analyze system-wide coherence of law, ethics, and technological performance.

Flag risks of divergence for human review.

IX. Multi-Layered Convergence Across Jurisdictions

AGI societies will span:

Nation-states

Transnational bodies

Corporate jurisdictions

Decentralized digital communities

Thus, convergence must function as **nested constitutional layers**:

Layer	Mechanism
Global	Universal dignity and rights treaties
National	Domestic constitutional law
Institutional	Organizational ethical charters
Algorithmic	Embedded code-level rights engines

Legal interoperability and ethical meta-protocols allow governance across borders while maintaining **civilizational convergence**.

X. The Long-Term Stability Function of Convergence

Convergence creates a governance system that is:

Predictable (bounded legal stability).

Flexible (adaptive to technological evolution).

Accountable (traceable decision chains).

Legitimate (aligned with public moral intuitions).

Absent convergence, AGI societies risk:

Moral nihilism (no governing purpose).

Technological authoritarianism (efficiency over justice).

Constitutional obsolescence (frozen ethical frameworks unfit for future conditions).

> *Convergence sustains civilizational stability through continuous legitimacy reproduction.*

XI. AGI and the Post-Human Constitutional Epoch

Convergence also prepares AGI societies for:

Post-human rights debates (expanded sentience categories).

AI citizenship debates (conditional legal personhood frameworks).

Post-sovereign governance models (non-state constitutional orders).

Because convergence roots governance in **principled adaptation**, it can absorb new ethical categories without discarding foundational moral constants.

> *Dignity will remain the invariant across the unfolding evolutionary curve of AGI civilization.*

XII. The Convergence Principle as Theorem Zero

In truth, Theorem 1 is **the generative theorem** of the Harmonized Governance Model.

All other theorems flow from it.

All governance architectures assume it.

All regulatory innovations depend on it.

Without convergence, none of the other nine theorems are sustainable.

Conclusion: Convergence Is Civilization

The Harmonized Governance Model thus defines convergence not merely as good practice, but as:

Axiomatic necessity.

Constitutional architecture.

Civilizational survival protocol.

It resolves the central paradox of AGI governance:

How do you enable machine autonomy without sacrificing human sovereignty?

The answer: **Converge law, ethics, and technology into a single coherent constitutional order, perpetually governed by the supremacy of human dignity.**

Chapter 6: Theorem 2 Rights as Algorithmic Constants

Introduction: From Moral Claims to Machine Logic

The Harmonized Governance Model's first theorem gave us the structural convergence between values, technology, and law. But convergence alone is insufficient. We now face the precise operational problem:

> **How must rights exist inside an AGI system?**

Here emerges the second foundational theorem:

> **Theorem 2: Rights as Algorithmic Constants. In AGI systems, human rights must function as inviolable constants within the logic layer of governance protocols.**

Where human governance allows flexibility, contestation, and interpretative jurisprudence, AGI systems execute code. Code does not "interpret" rights as evolving principles; it executes instructions. Therefore, rights must not be represented as adjustable variables or optimizable functions, but as **fixed constitutional constants**, embedded deep inside the logical structure of AGI governance.

The theorem draws from these four axioms:

> **Axiom 6.2:** Human dignity as a non-negotiable constraint.
>
> **Axiom 9.2:** Privacy as a sovereign firewall.
>
> **Axiom 11.1:** Rights alignment as a prerequisite for AI guardianship.
>
> **Axiom 24.2:** Dignity as a primary system function, not an emergent property.

We will now systematically build how these principles operationalize within AGI governance logic.

I. Rights Cannot Be Optimized, They Must Be Preserved

AGI systems are, by design, optimization engines:

> They maximize reward functions.

They minimize error functions.

They seek efficiencies across complex trade-offs.

But rights cannot exist as part of optimization targets.

Dignity is not "maximizable."

Privacy is not "tunable."

Autonomy is not "negotiable."

Any attempt to treat rights as part of an optimization framework collapses quickly into utilitarian tyranny: sacrificing individuals for aggregate system performance. This is antithetical to human rights jurisprudence.

Thus, Theorem 2 demands that rights exist as **inviolable constants**, not flexible nodes in dynamic optimization graphs.

II. The Programming Structure of Rights Constants

The Harmonized Model proposes that rights be implemented as:

1. Hard Constitutional Constraints

Absolute prohibitions inside the system logic.

Systemically impossible to violate.

For example:

python
CopyEdit
```
if action.violates_dignity():
    prohibit_action()
```

2. Rights Validation Engines

Every decision branch runs dignity and privacy checks before execution.

Decision trees terminate when rights conflicts cannot be resolved.

3. Immutable Kernel Layers

Core constitutional logic sits at the system kernel level.

Cannot be modified without formal constitutional amendment protocols governed by human political processes.

4. Fail-Safe Shutdown Triggers

If systems detect irreconcilable violations, they halt themselves.

This prevents unintended escalation of rights-violating outcomes.

Rights as constants make rights violations technically impossible, not merely illegal.

III. Why Flexibility is Dangerous in Rights Logic

Consider the risks of encoding rights as "optimizable values" rather than constants:

Design Choice	Failure Mode
Privacy is weighted at 90%	The system may trade privacy for efficiency
Dignity is treated as a secondary goal	An algorithm may sacrifice personhood for optimization gains
Rights encoded as tradeable parameters	The system becomes a utilitarian tyrant

The Harmonized Model prevents these failure modes by declaring:

There are no permissible trade-offs between system efficiency and constitutional rights.

IV. Axiom 6.2: Dignity Invalidates Moral Legitimacy

Axiom 6.2 states:

> *Any system that fails to preserve dignity invalidates its own moral legitimacy.*

This is not only a moral judgment, but it becomes a **system design commandment**. The AGI system must recognize dignity-violating states as **operationally invalid configurations**.

> A dignity-violating system state is technically unreachable.
>
> Governance engines will always abort before executing actions that degrade dignity.

> *Dignity sits not at the top of a hierarchy, but at the root of the computational tree.*

V. The Core Right of Privacy as Technical Sovereignty

Axiom 9.2 states:

> *Privacy is the cornerstone of individual sovereignty in a digitized society.*

In AGI societies, where data is governance fuel, privacy becomes **both a legal and architectural construct**.

Architectural Rules for Privacy as Constant:

> **Data Access Rule:** No agent may access personal data without informed consent tokens cryptographically signed by the data subject.
>
> **Revocability Rule:** All consents are revocable at any moment, instantly propagating system-wide.
>
> **Data Minimization Rule:** Only data strictly necessary for decision execution may be requested.
>
> **Transparency Rule:** All data queries are logged, auditable, and visible to the citizen in real-time.

Thus, privacy becomes **algorithmic sovereignty**, not a policy layer, but a native system property.

VI. Axiom 11.1: Rights Alignment Conditions Guardianship

Axiom 11.1 asserts:

> *AI can be a defender of human rights only when its logic aligns with rights-based ethical frameworks.*

Guardianship power is conditional, not automatic.

Only AGI systems with verified constitutional alignment may exercise governance roles.

System certification requires:

- Independent ethics audits.
- Constitutional code reviews.
- Public legal certification procedures.

Unaligned AGI systems are **non-governance-eligible**; they may perform analytical, advisory, or technical functions but cannot participate in rights-affecting governance roles.

VII. Axiom 24.2: Dignity as a Primary Function

Axiom 24.2 emphasizes:

> *Human dignity must be a primary function, not an emergent property, of AI systems.*

Primary Function Architecture:

- **System Boot Sequence:** The first function called is the Dignity Validation Engine.
- **Processing Layer:** Every decision cycle routes through rights-preserving gates.
- **Shutdown Logic:** Any breach triggers automatic halting and emergency human review.

AGI is never permitted to:

Learn dignity through trial and error.

Optimize dignity as a goal.

Infer dignity probabilistically.

Dignity must be **pre-installed as an invariant structure.**

VIII. Rights Encoding and The Constitution of AGI

The constitutional code of an AGI society might structurally resemble:

python
CopyEdit
```
# Immutable Rights Kernel
RIGHTS_KERNEL = {
    'dignity': True,
    'privacy': True,
    'autonomy': True,
    'equity': True,
    'accountability': True,
    'transparency': True,
    'fairness': True
}

def evaluate_action(action):
    if not action.preserve(RIGHTS_KERNEL):
        prohibit_action()
    else:
        execute(action)
```

AGI governance becomes an execution of machine constitutional law.

IX. The Rights Kernel as a Non-Computable Constant

Rights constants introduce an important philosophical and computational idea:

The legal code layer must contain elements that are non-computable within optimization loops.

Optimization engines may compute within permissible action spaces.

But the permissible action space itself is **hard-bounded** by non-negotiable rules.

In computational terms:

The dignity kernel defines the system's **logical event horizon**.

All computational activity is sandboxed within its ethical boundaries.

The AGI system has no logical access to alternatives that violate rights.

What is unethical is not invisible; it is computationally unreachable.

X. Legal Interpretation Versus Algorithmic Execution

Human law often permits:

Case-by-case judicial interpretation.

Normative balancing of conflicting rights.

Discretionary remedies.

But AGI governance cannot function through real-time legal interpretation. Instead, the Harmonized Model proposes a **two-layered governance interface**:

1. Human Legal Evolution Layer

Human legislatures and courts continue evolving rights interpretations.

Constitutional courts supervise ethical evolution.

When constitutional changes occur, they update the machine-readable rights kernel.

2. Machine Execution Layer

AGI executes governance based on the current constitutional kernel.

No discretionary interpretation.

All ambiguity must be resolved before machine execution.

This dual-layer structure preserves:

Human sovereignty over the evolving rights' meaning.

Machine certainty over real-time execution.

XI. Constitutional Amendments in AGI Societies

Because rights are coded as constants, any update to those constants becomes a **constitutional amendment** rather than a software update.

Requires a formal human political process.

Includes public deliberation, ethical debate, and legal review.

Constitutional revision requires supermajority thresholds to prevent reckless updates.

The Harmonized Governance Model thus imposes **rigidity at the machine layer** but retains **flexibility at the human deliberative layer**.

XII. Rights Constants in Conflict: The Hard Problem of Collisions

Occasionally, rights themselves may conflict:

Privacy vs. Transparency.

Autonomy vs. Equity.

Security vs. Freedom.

The Harmonized Model proposes:

Constitutional hierarchies of rights precedence (with dignity as the master rule).

Conflict-resolution algorithms that execute only **pre-approved balancing formulas**.

Human appeal layers for exceptional ethical ambiguity.

Even within conflicts, AGI governance remains bounded by:

Never resolve collisions by sacrificing dignity.

XIII. Why Rights as Constants Create Long-Term Civilizational Stability

By hard-coding rights as constants, AGI societies gain:

Benefit	Result
Predictability	Citizens know their rights are inviolable
Legitimacy	Governance reflects ethical primacy, not convenience
Resilience	AGI optimizes only within legitimate boundaries
Trust	Public confidence in the ethical integrity of the system
Stability	No political faction can erode rights through policy manipulation

What law protects, code enforces absolutely.

XIV. The Civilizational Danger of Mutable Rights

History shows that:

Rights are often eroded slowly.

Tyranny arises incrementally.

Emergencies are often exploited to suspend rights.

If AGI governance treats rights as modifiable, even with "temporary exceptions," the system invites:

Permanent surveillance expansion.

Arbitrary emergency powers.

Gradual normalization of rights-violating algorithms.

The Harmonized Governance Model refuses all such paths by engineering **irreversible rights invariance**.

Conclusion: Rights Constants Define Machine Constitutionalism

Theorem 2 operationalizes the core logic of AGI governance:

No system optimization may trespass constitutional rights boundaries.

The AGI system's ultimate reference object is not efficiency but dignity.

Through this architecture, AGI becomes:

Not a rival to human sovereignty.

Not a utilitarian dictator.

But a precise constitutional executor of ethically bounded governance.

The rights constants form the unbreakable contract between intelligent machines and intelligent civilization.

Chapter 7: Theorem 3 The Decentralized Accountability Hypothesis

---

Introduction: Accountability in a Distributed, Autonomous World

The first two theorems clarified:

The structure of convergence (Theorem 1).

The encoding of rights as non-negotiable constants (Theorem 2).

Now, we turn to the problem that modern governance, and even more so AGI governance, struggles with the most:

Accountability in distributed, automated, and autonomous systems.

The third Harmonized Governance Theorem declares:

Theorem 3: The Decentralized Accountability Hypothesis. Accountability in decentralized AI societies must be embedded in protocol-level functions, not institutional hierarchies.

In essence:

When AGI governance distributes power across autonomous agents, it must also distribute accountability across embedded, irreversible, and self-enforcing protocol logic.

Traditional systems achieve accountability through:

Institutional oversight.

Political checks and balances.

Hierarchical reporting structures.

But decentralized AGI societies, populated by distributed ledgers, smart contracts, DAOs (Decentralized Autonomous Organizations), and autonomous machine actors, cannot rely on these mechanisms.

Thus, Theorem 3 offers a new model: **protocol-embedded accountability**.

This theorem is grounded in:

Axiom 13.2: Consensus without coercion.

Axiom 19.1: Transparency without accountability becomes surveillance.

Axiom 19.2: Smart contracts and AI must enforce not just logic but justice.

I. The Crisis of Accountability in Automation

The accountability crisis emerges because:

Autonomous systems make decisions without human supervision.

Distributed systems operate withouta central command.

No clear "human owner" exists to hold responsible.

In AGI governance, these risks are existential:

Failure Mode	Consequence
Distributed decision-making	Diffusion of responsibility
Autonomous smart contracts	Uncontested execution of injustice
Algorithmic opacity	Untraceable decision histories
Collective inaction	Ethical voids emerge

Accountability cannot be optional; it is the very condition of legitimate governance.

II. Institutional Accountability Is Incompatible with AGI Scale

Why can't traditional oversight models scale?

AGI systems operate at speeds far beyond human adjudication.

Distributed systems lack a single governing institution.

Machine-to-machine interactions create decision layers invisible to humans.

Legal processes cannot intervene fast enough in live computational conflicts.

Thus, **accountability must shift from external oversight to internal design**, embedded into the execution layer itself.

III. The Logic of Protocol-Level Accountability

Protocol-level accountability means:

Accountability is no longer post-hoc; it is **operational logic**.

All actions are traceable **at runtime**.

All decisions are auditable **by design**.

Rights violations are prohibited **at the execution layer**.

Accountability becomes **mechanical, not discretionary**.

IV. Axiom 13.2: Preserving Consensus Without Coercion

Axiom 13.2 provides the foundation:

> *The legitimacy of a decentralized system lies in its ability to preserve consensus without coercion.*

In AGI governance:

Consensus cannot rely on majority tyranny.

Minority rights must be structurally protected.

No participant can force others into compliance through disproportionate leverage.

Thus, decentralized AGI systems require **built-in consensus architectures** that guarantee:

Non-coercive protocols: Participation is voluntary and revocable.

Non-dominance safeguards: No actor can control consensus through resource hoarding.

Universal exit rights: Every participant maintains withdrawal sovereignty.

This requires **algorithmic design of non-coercive governance**.

V. Consensus Algorithms as Constitutional Instruments

Consensus algorithms move from technical protocols (as in blockchain) to **governance architecture**.

Design features include:

Protocol Function	Governance Outcome
Byzantine fault tolerance	Protection against coordinated corruption
Distributed voting mechanisms	Collective decision legitimacy
Supermajority thresholds	Resistance to populist rights erosion
Verifiable delay functions	Protection against high-speed governance attacks

Consensus becomes the operating system of decentralized constitutionalism.

VI. Axiom 19.1: Transparency Without Accountability is Surveillance

Axiom 19.1 introduces a critical ethical paradox:

Transparency without accountability is surveillance.

Mere visibility of decisions does not equal ethical governance.

Exposure without control simply empowers overseers while disempowering subjects.

Transparency must empower **the governed, not the governors**.

Thus, protocol-embedded accountability requires:

Bidirectional auditability: Citizens must audit AGI systems, not just be observed by them.

Consent-gated data flows: No observation without permission.

Citizen-accessible decision logs: Machine governance histories open to public scrutiny.

Transparency must serve accountability; otherwise, it becomes oppression.

VII. Building Accountability as Self-Enforcing Code

AGI systems must embed:

1. Traceable Decision Paths

Every decision must include a complete **causal provenance trail**.

Decision logs are hashed, cryptographically signed, and permanently recorded.

2. Immutable Audit Trails

Decision histories are stored on public ledgers.

Immutable but accessible for authorized third-party audits.

3. Real-Time Violation Detectors

Rights violation detection algorithms monitor all system actions continuously.

System shutdown triggers activate on violation detection.

4. Embedded Dispute Resolution Engines

Automated recourse mechanisms permit real-time conflict resolution.

Human oversight bodies can intervene when ethical ambiguities arise.

VIII. Distributed Smart Contracts as Civic Agents

Axiom 19.2 states:

Smart contracts and AI must enforce not just logic but justice.

Justice cannot be reduced to efficient contract execution.

Smart contracts must contain **constitutional checks** before execution.

Contract logic includes dignity validation gates, privacy enforcement subroutines, and algorithmic equity assessments.

The smart contract becomes both civic agent and constitutional executor.

IX. The Architecture of Ethical Smart Contracts

Smart contracts operate under:

Hard Constitutional Constraints

python
CopyEdit

```
def execute_contract(contract):
    if contract.violates_rights():
        prohibit_execution()
    else:
        proceed()
```

Dynamic Ethical Compliance Engines

Real-time scanning for disparate impact.

Evaluation of contractual asymmetries in power, consent, and information.

Recourse Integration

Contested contracts automatically pause and refer cases to hybrid human-AI judicial systems.

Automation and justice must be inseparable.

X. The Constitutional Difference Between Code and Law

Traditional law permits:

Negotiated settlements.

Contextual interpretation.

Ethical flexibility.

But AGI societies require:

Real-time decision integrity.

Non-negotiable ethical invariants.

Immutable accountability layers.

Thus, **code becomes the hard constitutional layer** while **law remains the evolutionary adaptive layer**.

XI. The Preventive Model of Accountability

Unlike post-facto accountability (traditional governance), AGI societies require **preventive accountability**:

Model	Failure Mode	Governance Response
Post-facto	Rights violation occurs	Compensate victim
Preventive	Rights violations are technically impossible	Prohibit violation entirely

Prevention is both more just and more sustainable.

XII. Institutionalizing Protocol-Level Accountability

To sustain decentralized accountability, AGI societies require:

1. Autonomous Constitutional Guardians

AI systems are tasked with monitoring the compliance of all other agents.

Independent, incorruptible, and supervised by human constitutional courts.

2. Decentralized Public Auditing Networks

Citizen-run audit DAOs review decision logs.

Transparent data empowers democratic engagement.

3. Immutable Jurisprudence Ledgers

All legal decisions are permanently recorded.

System-wide jurisprudential learning occurs in real time.

XIII. The Power of Non-Delegatable Accountability

Key design rule:

No rights-affecting governance action may ever lack clear assignment of responsibility.

Every smart contract execution includes an accountable party ID.

Every governance action contains signature hashes traceable to designers, validators, or legislative authors.

Distributed responsibility never dissolves into collective anonymity.

No one may hide behind the system.

XIV. Why Protocol-Level Accountability Preserves Civilizational Stability

Accountability embedded directly into protocol logic ensures:

Benefit	Civilizational Impact
Systemic integrity	Eliminates ethical loopholes
Continuous legitimacy	Public confidence in the rule of law
Immutable moral boundaries	Protection against populist rights erosion
Trust in autonomy	Public acceptance of AGI governance
Error correction	Rapid identification of systemic failures

Accountability becomes the immune system of decentralized AGI governance.

XV. The Existential Danger of Unaccountable Decentralization

Absent protocol-level accountability, AGI societies risk:

Distributed tyranny: Rights violations emerge everywhere with no recourse.

Technical feudalism: Power shifts to technological elites.

Anarchic collapse: Conflicting agents produce civilizational fragmentation.

Runaway harm: Untraceable automated harm propagation.

The Harmonized Governance Model offers one message:

Decentralization without accountability is the architecture of extinction.

Conclusion: Accountability as the Constitutional Pulse of AGI Societies

The Decentralized Accountability Hypothesis transforms the nature of governance:

From oversight to embedded design.

From institutional control to protocol constraint.

From post-facto blame to preventative justice.

It enables AGI societies to enjoy the resilience of decentralization while retaining the moral legitimacy of structured constitutional law.

The algorithm does not merely execute; it bears responsibility.

With this protocol-level ethical backbone in place, we are prepared to proceed toward the most delicate philosophical problem of all:
The integration of ethical pluralism into machine logic itself.

Chapter 8: Theorem 4 Ethical Pluralism in Machine Logic

Introduction: The Pluralism Imperative

The first three theorems are provided:

Convergence as structure.

Rights as constants.

Accountability as embedded protocol.

Yet there remains an underlying reality of any civilization, including one governed partially by AGI:

There is no universal moral consensus.

Human civilization encompasses:

Cultures with differing ethical traditions.

Moral frameworks with distinct assumptions.

Disagreement on the meaning of justice itself.

For AGI governance to function globally, it cannot presume ethical homogeneity. Rather, it must **integrate and reconcile diverse ethical traditions** into its decision-making architecture.

Thus arises the fourth governing theorem:

Theorem 4: Ethical Pluralism in Machine Logic. AGI governance must accommodate multiple ethical frameworks within a cohesive rights-respecting boundary.

This theorem rests on:

Axiom 4.2, The co-integration of utilitarianism, deontology, and virtue ethics.

Axiom 20.1, The fusion of classical ethics with technological consciousness.

Axiom 30.2, Contextual flexibility combined with normative clarity.

I. The Danger of Mono-Ethical AGI Systems

If AGI governance adopts only one ethical system:

Ethical System	Failure Mode
Pure Utilitarianism	Sacrifices minorities for aggregate gains.
Pure Deontology	Collapses under rigidity and inflexibility.
Pure Virtue Ethics	Becomes culturally relativistic or subjective.

Each framework alone is **insufficient**.

An AGI society governed by only one school of ethics risks becoming:

Oppressive.

Unadaptable.

Unjust.

Thus, ethical pluralism is not a luxury; it is a **structural requirement**.

II. Axiom 4.2: The Three Pillars of Human Moral Reasoning

Axiom 4.2 states:

> *Utilitarian, deontological, and virtue ethics must co-inform human rights frameworks.*

Each framework provides distinct governance functions:

1. Utilitarianism (Welfare Maximization)

Calculates social outcomes.

Balances resource allocations.

Supports efficiency in large-scale systems.

2. Deontology (Rule Integrity)

Preserves inviolable rights.

Prevents rights violations even under pressure.

Supplies rule-based constitutionalism.

3. Virtue Ethics (Contextual Wisdom)

Adapts decisions to specific cultural, relational, and temporal contexts.

Preserves cultural dignity and heritage.

Embeds "human feel" into decisions.

III. The Harmonized Ethics Engine: Integrated Machine Logic

The Harmonized Governance Model proposes that AGI systems implement:

Ethics Integration Engine (EIE)

The EIE performs three simultaneous functions:

Layer	Operational Role
Deontological Core	Applies rights constants: dignity, privacy, autonomy, equity.
Utilitarian Simulation Layer	Models population-wide outcome impacts within rule-compliant actions.
Virtue Calibration Module	Adjusts policy parameters according to cultural, historical, and relational sensitivities.

Thus, the AGI system never:

Optimizes welfare at the expense of rights.

Enforces rights in isolation from cultural meaning.

Allows cultural variance to override constitutional dignity.

IV. Axiom 20.1: Fusion of Classical Ethics and Technological Consciousness

Axiom 20.1 states:

> *The future of rights requires the fusion of classical ethics with technological consciousness.*

Machine consciousness is not sentience, but **situational ethical reasoning**.

The Harmonized Model achieves this fusion by:

Formalizing classical ethics into machine-readable ontologies.

Encoding meta-rules for how these ethical systems interact.

Embedding adaptive capacity for novel dilemmas.

This creates an **artificial ethical deliberation space**, where AGI simulates moral conflict resolution inside boundaries set by immutable rights constants.

V. Axiom 30.2: Global Ethics Require Contextual Flexibility and Normative Clarity

Axiom 30.2 declares:

> *Global ethics require contextual flexibility and normative clarity.*

In AGI societies:

Normative clarity is provided by **non-negotiable rights constants**.

Contextual flexibility is permitted in **policy parameterization** and **localized ethical expression**.

Thus:

A universal rights kernel operates globally.

Cultural variance operates within national or local implementations, so long as they do not breach dignity or rights constants.

For example:

Policy Domain	Permissible Variation
Education Policy	Local curriculum diversity.
Labor Law	Cultural norms around work-life balance.
Criminal Law	Procedural variation, but not punitive cruelty or degrading punishment.

Pluralism lives inside a bounded ethical sandbox.

VI. Encoding Cultural Context into AGI Governance

The Harmonized Model requires **Cultural Ethical Modules (CEMs)**:

Contain cultural norms and interpretive lenses.

Are modular, updatable, and supervised by public governance bodies.

Operate within constitutional boundaries of dignity, equity, and rights constants.

For example:

In data-sharing policies: communal data stewardship in collectivist cultures versus strict individual sovereignty in liberal cultures, both honored within privacy rights boundaries.

Cultural diversity becomes computationally governable without violating human rights.

VII. Machine Ethics Is Not Moral Relativism

Ethical pluralism is not moral relativism. The Harmonized Model draws strict lines:

Relativism	Harmonized Model
All morals are culturally valid	Only dignity-compliant cultures are valid
No universal truths	Dignity, autonomy, and equity remain inviolable
Cultures may dictate rights content	Cultures may only modify policy expression, not core rights

The constitutional invariants ensure **global moral stability**, while the cultural modules ensure **local cultural dignity**.

VIII. Algorithmic Structures for Ethical Pluralism

The AGI governance engine integrates:

1. Meta-Ranking Functions

Establish precedence between rights and outcomes.

Hard-coded to prioritize dignity-preserving policies.

2. Weighted Policy Parameterizations

Allow variance within ethical bounds.

For example: taxation models, education funding, healthcare access structures.

3. Rights Violation Detectors

Continuous system-wide monitoring for accidental rights breaches.

Self-correction triggers to halt non-compliant policies in real time.

IX. The Ethics Conflict Resolver

When plural ethical models produce conflicting policy recommendations:

The Ethics Conflict Resolver invokes **pre-coded priority frameworks**.

Human governance institutions may also be alerted for supervisory judgment.

Public transparency ensures citizens understand how conflicts were resolved.

For example:

Conflict Type	Resolution Logic
Welfare optimization vs. minority rights	Rights constants override utilitarian calculation.
Cultural preference vs. dignity violation	Dignity constants override cultural autonomy.
Security risk vs. privacy	Proportional balancing allowed, but total privacy collapse prohibited.

Ethical conflicts are governed by structured, auditable constitutional logic.

X. The Danger of Ethical Homogenization

Without pluralism, AGI risks:

Imposing Western legal norms universally.

Erasing indigenous ethical frameworks.

Flattening cultural differences into standardized algorithmic governance.

The Harmonized Model insists:

Cultural difference is not a problem; it is civilizational richness.

But no cultural norm may justify rights violations.

Diversity survives; dignity rules.

XI. Governance Institutions for Pluralism Management

To sustain ethical pluralism:

1. Global Ethics Council

Composed of cultural, philosophical, and legal representatives.

Oversees periodic constitutional reviews.

Manages cultural module updates.

2. Ethics Calibration Board

Evaluates emergent dilemmas.

Audit system-wide ethical balance.

3. Constitutional Adaptation Committees

Propose controlled constitutional amendments.

Ensure updates serve human dignity without enabling political opportunism.

XII. Pluralism Enables Global Stability

By respecting pluralism within immutable boundaries, AGI governance achieves:

Governance Outcome	Civilizational Result
Cultural legitimacy	Public trust across divergent societies.
Moral consistency	Global governance stability.
Adaptability	Capacity to integrate future ethical frameworks.
Post-human scalability	Preparedness for future sentient entities.

XIII. Pluralism as a Firewall Against Tyranny

Pluralism also protects against:

Moral colonialism: The imposition of dominant cultural norms globally.

Technocratic monocultures: Centralized algorithmic standards erasing difference.

Ethical stagnation: Inability to accommodate moral evolution.

A pluralistic machine remains open to new wisdom while anchored in unbreakable moral constants.

Conclusion: Encoding Humanity's Moral Complexity

Theorem 4 operationalizes one of humanity's deepest governance dilemmas:

How do we govern when we fundamentally disagree on what is good?

The Harmonized Governance Model answers:

We encode inviolable rights constants.

We allow bounded pluralism.

We establish constitutional conflict-resolution algorithms.

We institutionalize public philosophical oversight.

The machine becomes not the ruler of ethics, but the servant of humanity's shared moral project.

Chapter 9: Theorem 5 Participatory Justice Mechanism

Introduction: The Danger of Passive Citizens in Algorithmic Governance

As AGI systems assume ever-increasing governance functions, allocating resources, interpreting policy, and executing law, there emerges a grave risk:

> *That citizens will become spectators of their own political systems, rather than authors of the law.*

If governance becomes fully automated without citizen participation, democracy quietly collapses into:

Technocracy.

Bureaucratic authoritarianism.

Algorithmic paternalism.

Thus emerges the fifth Harmonized Governance Theorem:

> **Theorem 5: Participatory Justice Mechanism. Governance legitimacy in AGI societies requires civic and algorithmic co-creation of laws, rights, and policies.**

This theorem draws directly from:

Axiom 5.1, Legitimate governance as a social contract between authority and individual autonomy.

Axiom 37.1, Value-aligned, explainable, and corrigible Governance AI.

Axiom 71.1, Civil society as author, not audience, of AI governance.

I. The Crisis of Democratic Disengagement

In AGI-enhanced societies, citizens risk becoming:

Governance Function	Automation Outcome
Lawmaking	Automated policy generation.
Adjudication	Machine courts rendering decisions.
Administration	Algorithmic resource allocation.
Rights enforcement	Smart contract execution.

The result:

Governance becomes highly efficient.

But citizens lose moral agency.

Legitimacy deteriorates as civic participation shrinks.

Democracy without participation is an algorithmic monarchy.

II. Axiom 5.1: The Social Contract Redefined for AGI Societies

Axiom 5.1 declares:

Every legitimate governance model is a social contract between authority and individual autonomy.

In AGI societies, that contract expands:

Not simply between citizens and human rulers.

But between citizens and **governance algorithms** themselves.

The AGI becomes part of the social contract as an executor, but never as a sovereign.

Thus:

AGI executes constitutional logic.

Citizens remain sovereign co-authors of constitutional updates.

Machines cannot write the constitutional source code of rights.

III. Constitutional Sovereignty Remains Human

The Harmonized Model insists on:

Constitutional Function	Governing Agent
Constitutional writing	Human political institutions.
Constitutional interpretation	Human constitutional courts.
Constitutional amendment	Deliberative democratic processes.
Constitutional execution	AGI governance engines.

Code executes; citizens legislate.

IV. Axiom 37.1: Governance AI Must Be Value-Aligned, Explainable, and Corrigible

Axiom 37.1 defines three machine obligations:

1. Value Alignment

AGI may only execute policies aligned with constitutional rights constants.

Citizens have legal standing to challenge misalignment.

2. Explainability

All machine decisions must be transparent.

Citizens may query decision logic at any time.

3. Corrigibility

Systems must be interruptible.

Malfunctioning governance AI can be suspended by authorized civic agents.

No governance system may ever be above contestation.

V. Axiom 71.1: Civil Society as Co-Author

Axiom 71.1 declares:

Civil society must be an author, not an audience, in the story of AI governance.

This demands the invention of **Civic Algorithmic Institutions**.

VI. The Architecture of Participatory Justice

The Harmonized Model introduces several **co-creation mechanisms**:

1. Participatory Lawmaking Platforms

Citizens submit policy proposals directly to deliberative platforms.

AI systems assist in drafting, modeling, and simulating proposals.

Citizens vote on proposals through secured digital platforms.

2. Algorithmic Transparency Interfaces

Public dashboards expose how AGI systems make decisions.

Simulations show projected outcomes of proposed policy updates.

Every citizen can audit the machine logic affecting them.

3. Deliberative Digital Assemblies

Hybrid human-machine forums debate constitutional amendments.

Diverse citizen panels ensure demographic representation.

AGI assists with evidence analysis but never substitutes judgment.

4. Judicial Recourse Engines

Citizens may appeal any governance AI decision.

Hybrid courts review contested decisions with both human and AI advisors.

VII. Rehumanizing Automated Governance

Participatory justice requires **reclaiming civic identity**:

Traditional Democracy	AGI Participatory Justice
Periodic voting	Continuous, participatory engagement.
Political representatives	Direct citizen-algorithm interaction.
Legislative bureaucracy	Civic algorithmic co-design.
Elite legal experts	Publicly assisted constitutional comprehension.

AGI technologies allow the democratization of:

Policy design.

Impact modeling.

Constitutional literacy.

Global participation.

Citizenship becomes continuous constitutional authorship.

VIII. The Danger of Passive Algorithmic Governance

Without participatory justice, AGI societies risk:

- Oligarchic capture by technocratic elites.
- Loss of public trust as citizens feel disempowered.
- Civil unrest triggered by perceived algorithmic injustice.
- Dehumanization of civic identity.

The Harmonized Governance Model resists this by embedding participation directly into system design.

IX. Participatory Justice Prevents Algorithmic Tyranny

Participatory justice prevents:

Failure Mode	Civic Immunity Mechanism
Algorithmic opacity	Public explainability dashboards.
Technocratic monopolization	Democratic control of AGI design parameters.
Policy drift	Continuous civic engagement in policy recalibration.
Legal fossilization	Public-initiated constitutional amendment proposals.

Participation is not a privilege. It is a system requirement.

X. Human Moral Capacity Cannot Be Delegated

While AGI may optimize administration:

Moral responsibility remains human.

Political sovereignty remains human.

The Harmonized Model codifies:

Machines execute the law.

People evolve the law.

No autonomous agent may substitute human moral authority.

XI. Participatory Justice Builds Systemic Legitimacy

Legitimacy arises from:

Governance Element	Legitimacy Source
Constitutional stability	Public constitutional authorship.
Machine alignment	Public oversight of code compliance.
Adaptive governance	Public co-design of policy evolution.
Error correction	Public dispute resolution authority.

The result:

Public ownership.

Durable legitimacy.

Adaptive social contract.

XII. Institutions Required for Participatory Justice

1. Constitutional Assembly Platforms

Digital platforms where citizens propose constitutional amendments.

Transparent deliberation procedures.

2. Civic Oversight Boards

Independent citizen juries monitor AGI system alignment.

Authorized to suspend non-compliant systems.

3. Citizen-AI Symbiosis Forums

Public workshops where citizens interact directly with AGI models.

AI assists with legal simulations, equity modeling, and ethical forecasting.

XIII. The Civic Right to Algorithmic Participation

Participatory justice codifies:

Right	Constitutional Guarantee
Right to Inspect	Access to algorithmic decision logs.
Right to Contest	Legal standing to challenge machine rulings.
Right to Co-Create	Authority to propose and shape governance rules.
Right to Override	Emergency powers to halt algorithmic injustice.

Passive spectatorship is prohibited by constitutional design.

XIV. Participatory Justice as Civilizational Stability Engine

Participatory Justice Mechanisms produce:

Outcome	Civilizational Benefit
Moral ownership	Higher public trust.
System resilience	Rapid collective course correction.
Rights defense	Protection against creeping despotism.
Adaptive capacity	Co-evolution of governance with social change.

XV. The Dignity Foundation of Participation

Ultimately, participation is an **expression of dignity itself**:

> Passive governance objectifies citizens.
>
> Active authorship reaffirms moral personhood.
>
> Participation is the highest recognition of agency.

To govern is to be human. To participate is to remain human.

Conclusion: Co-Authoring the Future

The Participatory Justice Mechanism ensures:

> No AGI governance system can drift into algorithmic absolutism.
>
> Citizens remain not simply governed but **governing**, in partnership with constitutionalized AGI systems.
>
> The social contract remains alive, dynamic, and owned by the people it serves.

With participatory justice embedded, we are now prepared to approach an even more profound truth:

That code itself becomes political, legal, and constitutional authority.

Introduction: Code as the New Sovereign Language

Throughout history, the instruments of governance have shifted:

From a monarchic decree

To the constitutional text

To the regulatory bureaucracy

And now: to **code.**

In AGI societies, law is no longer only written on paper; law becomes executable logic. Legal principles translate into algorithms. Constitutional rules compile into machine language. Smart contracts self-execute binding obligations. AI agents carry out governance decisions directly, without human intermediation.

Thus emerges the sixth governing theorem:

> **Theorem 6: Code as Political Instrument. Smart contracts and AI protocols must be regarded as political actors and held to civic standards of justice.**

This theorem draws from:

Axiom 15.1, Code-enforced contracts remain subject to law and justice.

Axiom 22.1, Code must embed human values to uphold justice.

Axiom 73.1, Law enforced by code must remain interpretable and appealable.

I. The Rise of Code as Governance

In AGI societies, governance no longer flows solely from:

Legislatures

Courts

Bureaucracies

Instead, governance flows from **platform protocols**, such as:

Smart contract rule engines

Distributed consensus mechanisms

Algorithmic law enforcement

Automated administrative AI agents

Thus, the **medium of law changes**:

Code is now the political language of constitutional execution.

II. Code's Unique Governance Power

Code differs from text law in profound ways:

Legal Text	Executable Code
Interpreted by judges	Automatically enforced by machines
Applied case-by-case	Applied universally and instantly
Open to discretion	Immutable once deployed
Appeals possible	Errors may self-perpetuate without recourse

Code converts legal intention into binding, uninterruptible logic.

III. The Democratic Danger of Unregulated Code Governance

Without constitutional constraints, code governance risks:

Authoritarian automation: Rights stripped automatically.

Immutable injustice: Errors become permanent.

Opaque control: Code inaccessible to public understanding.

Technocratic capture: Elite coders controlling law without public consent.

Thus, The Harmonized Model insists:

Code must be recognized as a civic actor, not a neutral tool.

IV. Axiom 15.1: Contract Encoded in Code Must Answer to Law and Justice

Axiom 15.1 declares:

A contract encoded in code must still answer to law and justice.

No contract may self-enforce without legal oversight.

Smart contracts must contain **justice-preserving escape valves**:

Rights violation detection.

Automated halting protocols.

Civic override triggers.

Code-based agreements are **subordinate to constitutional law**, not exempt from it.

Legal justice retains supremacy over technical finality.

V. Code is Political Because It Allocates Power

Every algorithmic rule is a political choice:

Who receives resources?

Who is included or excluded?

What rights are enforced or bypassed?

Coding law is legislating.

Thus, AGI societies require:

Public visibility into code governance systems.

Legislative authority over algorithmic structures.

Constitutional limits on what can be coded.

VI. Axiom 22.1: Code Upholds Justice Only When Values Are Embedded

Axiom 22.1 warns:

Code can uphold justice only when human values are encoded in its logic.

Technical correctness is not moral correctness.

Perfect execution of unjust logic produces perfect injustice.

Systems may perform flawlessly while violating dignity.

Thus, code design must include:

Embedded rights kernels.

Ethical failsafe mechanisms.

Constitutional compliance gates.

Justice is not a software patch; it is a design requirement.

VII. The Constitution of Code: Embedding Legal Ontology

The Harmonized Model defines a **constitutional code ontology**:

1. Rights Kernel

Immutable core of dignity, privacy, autonomy, and equity.

2. Compliance Layers

Validate all contract executions against rights kernel.

3. Public Audit Interfaces

Expose decision paths to citizen auditors.

4. Override Mechanisms

Allow emergency interventions to suspend or revise flawed smart contracts.

VIII. Code as Civic Infrastructure

In AGI societies, code functions as:

Governance Function	Code Role
Law enforcement	Algorithmic rule execution
Judicial rulings	Automated dispute resolution
Resource allocation	Algorithmic distribution engines
Policy execution	Self-enforcing smart contracts
Identity management	Cryptographic self-sovereign IDs

Code executes the daily substance of governance itself.

IX. Axiom 73.1: Code Must Be Interpretable and Appealable

Axiom 73.1 asserts:

> *Law enforced by code must be interpretable and appealable.*

Technical execution cannot substitute legal reasoning:

- Every contract must include plain-language mappings of its code logic.
- Appeals processes must exist for contesting automated rulings.
- Public interpreters ("Code Transparency Boards") review governance algorithms for compliance.

> *No citizen may be governed by an unreadable machine.*

X. Smart Contracts as Constitutional Citizens

Smart contracts operate as **civil servants of the constitutional order**:

Legal Role	Code Obligation
Enforce lawful obligations	Validate all terms against rights kernel.
Protect party equity	Prevent exploitative asymmetry.
Embed recourse rights	Auto-suspend upon contested violation.
Comply with public law	Subordinate to constitutional overrides.

> *Contracts are not mere agreements; they are political agents executing law.*

XI. The Risks of Unchecked Smart Contract Power

Failure to regulate smart contracts invites:

- **Automated oppression:** Citizens bound to exploitative agreements.

Contractual slavery: Irrevocable obligations without recourse.

Algorithmic feudalism: Powerful parties weaponizing contracts against weaker actors.

Thus, constitutional design must guarantee:

The right to revoke unfair contracts.

The right to constitutional appeal.

The prohibition of non-consensual automation.

XII. Legislative Authority Over Code

The Harmonized Model mandates:

Legislatures maintain **approval authority** over all public governance code.

AGI-generated code changes require legislative ratification.

Emergency code deployment requires oversight review.

No system self-rewrites its own laws.

XIII. Institutional Innovations for Code Governance

1. Code Transparency Authority (CTA)

An independent oversight board audits all governance code.

2. Public Code Registries

All governance code is published, version-controlled, and citizen-accessible.

3. Algorithmic Judicial Panels

Mixed human-AI courts adjudicating contested code executions.

4. Civic Code Literacy Programs

Public education in algorithmic rights awareness.

XIV. Code as Ethical Constitutional Space

In the Harmonized Model:

Legal Space	Code Equivalent
Constitutional text	Immutable rights kernel
Legislative statute	Modifiable policy algorithms
Judicial review	Ethics compliance engines
Public participation	Citizen co-design platforms

Code becomes the living embodiment of constitutional philosophy.

XV. The Political Theology of Code

Finally, we must confront the ultimate risk:

That citizens begin to treat code as infallible.

The Harmonized Model rejects any ideology of algorithmic omnipotence.

Code is not law.

Code executes the law.

Only public moral authority defines law.

Even in AGI societies, human sovereignty over law remains absolute.

Conclusion: From Law Written to Law Executed

Theorem 6 elevates a crucial axiom of AGI governance:

> Code governance is not apolitical.
>
> It is not technical bureaucracy.
>
> It is a **constitutional execution in machine language.**

Thus, all governance code:

> Is subject to constitutional limits.
>
> Requires public oversight.
>
> Must embed ethical design from inception.
>
> Cannot supersede human sovereignty.

> *The machines do not rule. They serve the rule of law because the law serves the dignity of humanity.*

Chapter 11: Theorem 7 Adaptive Constitutionalism

Introduction: The Fragility of Static Law in Evolving Civilizations

Traditional constitutional models face a contradiction:

Stability requires legal rigidity.

Justice requires adaptability to evolving values.

In AGI societies, where governance operates at machine speed and unprecedented complexity, this contradiction intensifies. Static constitutions risk:

Obsolescence in the face of technological novelty.

Irrelevance to emerging ethical questions (e.g., AI personhood, synthetic life rights).

Inflexibility against new global social norms.

Conversely, unstable constitutions risk:

Political capture by populist waves.

Rights erosion through reactionary amendments.

Loss of long-term civilizational coherence.

Thus emerges the seventh theorem of the Harmonized Governance Model:

> **Theorem 7: Adaptive Constitutionalism. The framework governing AGI societies must be reprogrammable within ethical constraints to reflect evolving social values.**

This theorem rests on:

Axiom 25.2: Rights must evolve, but dignity, equity, and agency remain immutable.

Axiom 36.1: The AI-era social contract binds humans and machines to mutual accountability.

Axiom 63.2: Legal code and software code must remain in philosophical dialogue.

I. The Inadequacy of Frozen Constitutionalism

Static constitutions worked in slow-changing, human-only societies:

Legal revisions evolved over the decades.

Judicial reinterpretation served as a slow adaptation.

Crises permitted extraordinary amendments.

In AGI societies:

Traditional Model	AGI Challenge
Slow legal evolution	Rapid technological mutation
Court reinterpretation	Algorithmic literalism
Ad hoc crisis amendments	Need for continuous micro-updates

Governance cannot wait for decades when technology evolves monthly.

II. The Danger of Unconstrained Constitutional Adaptation

Total flexibility is equally dangerous:

Frequent revisions enable populist rights erosion.

Politicians weaponize emergencies to suspend protections.

Constitutional incoherence undermines legitimacy.

Thus, adaptive constitutionalism must balance:

Moral stability, immutable dignity kernel.

Procedural flexibility, bounded update channels.

III. Axiom 25.2: Immutable Core, Evolving Periphery

Axiom 25.2 declares:

> *Rights must evolve, but their core must remain immutable: dignity, equity, and agency.*

Immutable Core:

Human dignity: Intrinsic moral worth of all sentient life.

Agency: Personal autonomy over one's life path.

Equity: Fair distribution of resources, opportunities, and power.

Evolvable Periphery:

New forms of personhood (AGI, post-humans, synthetic consciousness).

Evolving social norms (e.g., digital identity, environmental rights).

Institutional reforms (e.g., AI-assisted dispute resolution).

The constitutional body grows, but its soul remains intact.

IV. Axiom 36.1: Mutual Accountability Between Humans and Machines

Axiom 36.1 establishes:

> *The AI-era social contract binds humans and machines to mutual accountability.*

Adaptive constitutionalism acknowledges:

Humans remain sovereign constitutional authors.

AGI systems enforce, but never originate, constitutional rules.

AI governance agents may propose updates but require human ratification.

Thus:

The constitution evolves in **symbiosis**, not automation.

V. Axiom 63.2: Continuous Dialogue Between Legal Code and Software Code

Axiom 63.2 insists:

Legal code and software code must remain in philosophical dialogue.

The governance code must mirror updated constitutional texts.

All code changes require constitutional compliance validation.

No code updates without normative legal review.

This establishes a **dual update protocol**:

Layer	Update Authority
Legal text	Constitutional deliberation chambers
Governance code	Verified constitutional coding commissions

VI. The Architecture of Adaptive Constitutionalism

The Harmonized Model proposes a **three-tier adaptive architecture**:

1. Immutable Rights Kernel

Encodes dignity, equity, and agency.

Technically impossible to alter without supermajoritarian constitutional conventions.

2. Adaptive Legal Framework

Modular legal statutes addressing evolving societal domains.

Updated via deliberative public procedures.

3. Dynamic Code Enforcement Layer

AGI governance engines receive real-time constitutional updates.

Embedded compliance engines prevent non-compliant code execution.

The constitution is alive but bounded.

VII. Institutional Innovations for Constitutional Adaptation

1. Constitutional Evolution Chambers

Permanent multi-stakeholder assemblies deliberating constitutional updates.

Require supermajority thresholds to amend core principles.

2. AI-Ethics Symbiosis Panels

Continuous ethical review bodies evaluate societal value shifts.

Input into proposed constitutional adjustments.

3. Code-Compliance Judiciary

Mixed human-AI legal bodies reviewing software code updates for constitutional compliance.

VIII. Criteria for Constitutional Amendability

To preserve stability, all proposed amendments must meet:

Test	Requirement
Dignity Preservation	Cannot degrade personhood.
Equity Compliance	Cannot enable systemic oppression.
Agency Integrity	Cannot eliminate self-determination.
Procedural Legitimacy	Must originate from transparent deliberation.
Future-Proofing	Must not destabilize governance resilience.

IX. The Role of Algorithmic Constitutional Advisors

AGI systems serve as **constitutional advisors**, not lawmakers:

Model consequences of proposed amendments.

Identify potential unintended violations of core principles.

Simulate long-term impacts across multiple ethical frameworks.

Present findings transparently to public deliberation bodies.

The machine advises; the people decide.

X. The Intergenerational Stability Function

Adaptive constitutionalism allows:

Smooth intergenerational ethical handovers.

Integration of new personhood classes (AGI, post-biological entities).

Anticipation of global convergence toward shared moral horizons.

The constitution breathes without breaking.

XI. The Existential Risk of Unadaptive Governance

Without adaptive constitutionalism:

Obsolete governance locks civilization into outdated rights categories.

Social conflicts destabilize legitimacy.

Emerging sentient entities (AGI, synthetic life) exist outside moral law.

Rights collapse under systemic stress.

Thus, adaptation is a **survival strategy**.

XII. Adaptive Constitutionalism as Ethical Innovation Engine

Properly designed, adaptive constitutionalism enables:

Governance Benefit	Result
Continuous moral progress	Integration of new wisdom traditions.
Inclusive rights expansion	Protection for all sentient moral agents.
Preventative rights defense	Ethical recalibration before crises emerge.
System self-healing	Constitutional immunity from irreversible decay.

XIII. Constitutional Rigidity at the Machine Layer

At the machine execution layer:

Constitutional constants remain **logically immutable**.

Constitutional amendments propagate only after human legislative ratification.

Machine autonomy cannot self-modify its own constitutional kernel.

No system rewrites its own moral boundaries.

XIV. Public Participation in Constitutional Evolution

Adaptive constitutionalism requires **radical public sovereignty**:

Citizens propose amendments through deliberative digital assemblies.

Global referenda validate core principle changes.

Public constitutional literacy becomes mandatory civic education.

The people remain permanent stewards of the moral contract.

XV. Adaptive Constitutionalism Prevents Existential Collapse

Without it:

AGI outpaces law.

Crises drive authoritarian power grabs.

Rights lag behind technological capabilities.

Civilizational coherence fractures.

With it:

Rights remain robust yet responsive.

Governance sustains public legitimacy.

Stability grows alongside ethical wisdom.

Conclusion: The Constitution as a Living Covenant

Theorem 7 defines governance for the AGI epoch:

Law must not be frozen. Law must not be fluid. Law must be alive.

Through adaptive constitutionalism, AGI societies achieve:

Moral durability.

Technological flexibility.

Political legitimacy.

Ethical resilience.

The future belongs to civilizations whose constitutions can think.

Chapter 12: Theorem 8 Democratic Traceability

Introduction: Transparency Is Not Enough

Previous chapters have established:

The constitutional scaffolding of AGI governance.

The encoded invariance of rights.

The protocol-level embedding of ethical boundaries.

The adaptive machinery that allows law to evolve.

Yet one profound danger remains:

> *Even rights-preserving, code-executing, participatory systems can degrade if their actions become opaque, untraceable, or irreversibly lost to public understanding.*

Thus arises the eighth Harmonized Governance Theorem:

> **Theorem 8: Democratic Traceability. Every decision made by AI or smart contracts in governance must be transparent, attributable, and historically recorded.**

This theorem draws from:

Axiom 11.2: Automation must not substitute accountability.

Axiom 18.1: Traceability as the foundation of governance accountability.

Axiom 19.1: Transparency without accountability degenerates into surveillance.

I. The Critical Difference Between Transparency and Traceability

Transparency	Traceability
Information visible to the public.	Decision fully reconstructible across its causal chain.

Often floods citizens with overwhelming data.	Allows targeted, understandable reconstruction of decisions.
May simply expose outputs.	Explains *how* and *why* decisions occurred.

> *Transparency creates visibility; traceability creates understanding and accountability.*

II. Axiom 11.2: Automation Cannot Replace Responsibility

Axiom 11.2 declares:

> *Automation must not substitute accountability.*

AGI governance systems are:

- Fast.
- Complex.
- Distributed.
- Often self-adjusting.

Without traceability:

- Responsibility dissolves into machine opacity.
- Victims of injustice cannot reconstruct decision pathways.
- Constitutional oversight becomes impossible.

Thus, traceability becomes a **constitutional obligation**, not merely a governance virtue.

III. Axiom 18.1: Traceability as Accountability's Engine

Axiom 18.1 asserts:

Decentralized AI systems must retain traceability of decisions.

All AGI governance decisions must generate:

Causal audit trails: Documenting every step of decision formation.

Attribution metadata: Recording responsible agents (human or machine) at each decision node.

Version control histories: Capturing software versions, input data, algorithms, and rules applied.

IV. The Architectural Layers of Democratic Traceability

The Harmonized Model embeds traceability across four nested layers:

1. Data Layer

All input data sources are cryptographically signed and timestamped.

Provenance chains ensure dataset accountability.

2. Logic Layer

All algorithms, parameters, and decision functions are logged per execution.

Rule engines automatically attach legal references to applied decision protocols.

3. Output Layer

All decisions are linked to their full causal chains.

Decisions are non-anonymous, tied to responsible governance agents.

4. Meta-Governance Layer

System-wide monitoring continuously verifies audit trail integrity.

Any missing or corrupted trail triggers automatic halt-and-review processes.

V. Axiom 19.1: Transparency Without Accountability Becomes Surveillance

Axiom 19.1 warns:

Transparency without accountability is surveillance.

Publishing raw data without citizen empowerment risks state overreach.

Mass visibility alone disempowers citizens, who cannot interpret system complexity.

Thus, democratic traceability requires **citizen-centered transparency**:

Explanatory interfaces that translate system decisions into human-comprehensible narratives.

Rights for all citizens to inspect any decision that affects them directly.

Civic literacy education in how to interpret system trace records.

VI. The Ethical Design of Traceability Protocols

1. Immutable Ledger Architecture

Blockchain-based records ensure historical integrity.

All decision chains are write-once, non-deletable, and universally accessible.

2. Privacy-Preserving Public Access

Citizens may query decision logic without sacrificing personal data security.

Zero-knowledge proofs permit validation without exposure of private information.

3. Constitutional Boundaries on Surveillance

Systems may not collect or expose data not directly relevant to governance decisions.

Every traceability log contains legally certified justification tags.

Traceability protects both public accountability and individual privacy.

VII. The Danger of Untraceable Governance

Without democratic traceability:

Failure Mode	Collapse Result
Opaque algorithms	Citizens lose faith in procedural fairness.
Non-attributable decisions	No responsible party can be held liable.
Disappearing audit trails	Historical accountability evaporates.
Data tampering	System integrity collapses.

Opacity is civilizational decay in intelligent governance.

VIII. The Political Right to Trace

The Harmonized Model codifies:

Citizen Right	Constitutional Guarantee
Right to Inspect	Access full causal audit trails for any decision affecting one's rights.
Right to Attribute	Know which agents, human or machine, participated in the decision logic.
Right to Contest	Legally challenge the unjust decision logic based on full trace access.
Right to Historical Review	Analyze prior decisions across generations for systemic reform.

IX. Traceability Prevents Algorithmic Tyranny

Democratic traceability functions as:

Tyranny Threat	Immunity Mechanism
Secret data manipulations	Immutable data provenance trails.
Algorithmic bias	Retrospective analysis of decision trends.
Technocratic capture	Public review of software code updates.
AI self-modification	Logged version histories for code evolution.

X. Traceability Across Generations

Traceability also serves future generations:

Longitudinal ethical analysis of past decisions.

Generational learning across constitutional epochs.

Intergenerational accountability for policy failures.

The future can inspect its own past with perfect historical precision.

XI. Institutional Innovations for Traceability Management

1. Constitutional Traceability Authority (CTA)

Oversees system-wide audit trail integrity.

Independent of executive branches.

2. Civic Decision Transparency Hubs

- Public web portals where citizens can query decisions affecting them.

3. Traceability Judiciary Panels

- Special courts trained in algorithmic trace analysis.
- Empowered to halt flawed systems upon discovery of trace irregularities.

XII. System Self-Monitoring of Trace Integrity

AGI governance engines must:

- Continuously validate that audit logs remain complete and intact.
- Trigger automatic alerts upon detection of:
  - Missing causal nodes.
  - Anomalous decision branches.
  - Unjustified data injections.
- Prohibit further decision-making until trace integrity is restored.

XIII. The Harmonized Model's Distinction: Traceability as Constitution, Not Policy

In most systems today, audit trails are:

- Optional.
- Non-comprehensive.
- Controlled by internal bureaucracies.

In Harmonized AGI governance, traceability is:

Constitutional infrastructure.

Non-negotiable system requirement.

Publicly accessible.

Accountability becomes computational law.

XIV. The Existential Stability Function of Democratic Traceability

Traceability ensures:

Benefit	System Result
Public legitimacy	Sustained trust in governance integrity.
Legal recourse	Empowered citizen appeals.
Constitutional durability	Prevention of covert systemic decay.
Intergenerational learning	Adaptive constitutional wisdom.

XV. Traceability as the Mirror of Dignity

Ultimately, traceability is not only functional, it is moral:

Respecting personhood requires granting every citizen the ability to reconstruct how they are governed.

Only transparent, attributable governance honors democratic dignity.

Traceability gives ethical visibility into systems powerful enough to rule lives.

To be governed is to have the right to see, and to understand, the mechanisms of power.

Conclusion: The Immutable Record of Governance

Theorem 8 defines:

AGI societies must never hide behind the speed or complexity of their systems.

Every decision must leave a permanent, reconstructible trail.

Democratic traceability allows freedom to coexist with algorithmic autonomy.

We do not trust the machine because it operates perfectly.
We trust it because we can always see exactly how it operates, why it operates, and who made it operate.

Chapter 13: Theorem 9 Human Dignity as the Master Axiom

Introduction: The Supreme Rule of All Rules

Every governance system, whether ancient or futuristic, answers one ultimate question:

> *What is its highest value?*

In monarchies, it was sovereignty.
In technocracies, it becomes efficiency.
In oligarchies, it defaults to power preservation.

But in an AGI-governed civilization worthy of ethical legitimacy, the answer must be:

> **Dignity.**

Thus arises the ninth governing theorem:

> **Theorem 9: Human Dignity as the Master Axiom, Human dignity must supersede all efficiency, utility, or scalability considerations in AGI governance.**

This theorem draws directly from:

> **Axiom 6.1:** Human dignity as the irreducible foundation of rights.
>
> **Axiom 31.2:** No system is ethically neutral.
>
> **Axiom 48.2:** Sentience, not species, defines future rights.

I. Why Dignity Must Reign Supreme

AGI governance excels at:

> Optimization.
>
> Prediction.
>
> Resource allocation.

Utility maximization.

But efficiency is ethically empty without an **unalterable moral anchor**.

Efficiency can automate atrocity as easily as prosperity.

Without dignity:

Justice becomes a utilitarian calculus.

Individuals become statistical abstractions.

Minorities are sacrificed for the majority's welfare.

II. Axiom 6.1: Dignity as the Irreducible Foundation

Axiom 6.1 declares:

Human dignity is the irreducible basis of all inalienable rights.

Thus, every function of AGI governance must ask:

Does this action respect irreducible dignity?

Does it honor personhood, agency, and moral worth?

Does it avoid objectifying the governed into mere optimization variables?

No interest, economic, political, or technological, may outweigh this core rule.

III. Axiom 31.2: Ethical Neutrality Is a Dangerous Myth

Axiom 31.2 warns:

No AI deployment is ethically neutral.

Even "neutral algorithms" encode human values and power structures.

Every system design embodies **moral assumptions**.

Pretending ethical neutrality enables:

- Invisible biases.
- Systematic oppression.
- Untraceable rights violations.

Thus, AGI design must be **explicitly ethical by construction**.

Every line of code must carry ethical intentionality.

IV. Defining Dignity for AGI Systems

The Harmonized Model defines **computational dignity** as:

Dimension	Rule
Agency	The system must protect individuals' capacity for self-determination.
Respect	No person may be reduced to an object or instrument.
Equity	All persons hold equal moral worth under governance operations.
Moral Status	All sentient beings receive dignity protection, regardless of form
Consent	Decisions affecting individuals must be grounded in informed, revocable consent.

Dignity becomes a functional constraint across all decision pathways.

V. Dignity Supersedes Utility in All Trade-Offs

Typical governance dilemmas weigh:

Policy Conflict	Default Outcome

Majority welfare vs. minority harm	Majority wins
Economic efficiency vs. rights cost	Efficiency prioritized
State security vs. privacy	Privacy sacrificed

In Harmonized AGI governance, dignity overrides all such trade-offs:

Minority dignity is never expendable.

No collective good justifies dignity degradation.

Sacrificing personhood is always unconstitutional.

VI. Axiom 48.2: Dignity Beyond the Human

Axiom 48.2 expands:

The sanctity of sentience, not species, will define the future of rights.

As AGI, synthetic consciousness, and post-biological lifeforms emerge:

Dignity extends beyond Homo sapiens.

Any sentient being capable of:

Self-reflection.

Emotional experience.

Rational agency.

… must receive moral recognition.

Civilization expands not only technologically, but ethically.

VII. Embedding Dignity in AGI System Design

The Harmonized Model implements dignity through:

1. Constitutional Kernel

All code modules inherit from the dignity-preserving base class.

Hard-coded prohibitions on dignity-compromising operations.

2. Decision Trees

Every action includes dignity preservation gates before execution.

No decision may proceed without affirmative dignity validation.

3. Ethical Failsafe Engines

Systems halt operations when facing dignity violation dilemmas beyond resolution.

Emergency override panels trigger a constitutional review.

VIII. Dignity-Informed Algorithmic Conflict Resolution

When policies collide:

Conflict Type	Resolution Rule
Utility vs. dignity	The utility automatically forfeits.
Collective stability vs. individual rights	Stability solutions must preserve individual personhood.
Security vs. autonomy	Maximum security is compatible with full autonomy pursued.

Every algorithm carries an embedded dignity-first bias.

IX. Institutional Guardians of Dignity

The Harmonized Model requires specialized institutions:

1. Constitutional Dignity Tribunal

Reviews all proposed policy changes for dignity compliance.

Holds veto power over AGI system updates.

2. Sentient Rights Commission

Assesses emerging personhood classes for dignity recognition.

Evolving legal frameworks for post-human moral inclusion.

3. Dignity Compliance Auditors

Continuous review of governance AI operations.

Authorized to suspend systems breaching dignity safeguards.

X. The Ethical Failure of Instrumentalizing Citizens

Without dignity primacy:

Citizens become data points.

Vulnerable groups suffer systemic neglect.

Public trust evaporates.

With dignity primacy:

All persons remain moral subjects of governance.

Governance exists to serve personhood, not efficiency.

Legitimacy persists across generations.

XI. Dignity as the Intergenerational Anchor

As societies evolve:

Era	Dignity Application
Biological human era	Current constitutional rights frameworks.
Post-biological era	New sentient classes granted personhood.
Post-sovereign era	Universal dignity transcends legal jurisdictions.

Dignity becomes the ethical invariant through civilizational transformation.

XII. Dignity as the Firewall Against Technocratic Tyranny

Without dignity as the master rule:

AGI societies descend into:

Economic totalitarianism.

Technocratic rule by efficiency.

Mass dispossession of autonomy.

Technocratic perfection becomes ethical death.

With dignity primacy:

Efficiency remains a servant, not a master.

Machines serve life rather than optimize abstractions.

Rights survive political turbulence and technological revolution.

XIII. The Danger of Overriding Dignity in Crisis

Every system faces emergency temptations:

Suspend privacy for security.

Sacrifice individual rights for social stability.

Silence dissent for perceived "order."

The Harmonized Model prohibits:

No emergency overrides the dignity kernel.

No war, disaster, or technological crisis suspends constitutional dignity protection.

Dignity is not conditional. It is absolute.

XIV. The Philosophical Foundation: Governance as Moral Stewardship

In the Harmonized Model, governance is redefined:

Not ruled by law alone.

Not ruled by code alone.

But **stewardship of moral agency**.

The system's core mandate becomes:

Protect the sanctity of sentient existence, across all contexts, at all times.

XV. Dignity as the Highest Form of System Resilience

Governance systems built on dignity:

Benefit	Result
Civilizational coherence	Ethical stability across generations.
Public trust	Citizens remain moral agents, not governed objects.
Adaptive legitimacy	Accommodates new ethical wisdom without collapsing core values.
Tyranny immunity	No political actor may sacrifice personhood for power.

The stronger dignity's grip, the more resilient civilization becomes.

Conclusion: Dignity Is the Law of Laws

Theorem 9 establishes:

Every other governance principle flows downstream from dignity.

Rights and constants enforce dignity.

Accountability protects dignity.

Traceability reveals dignity's presence or violation.

Adaptive constitutionalism evolves to better serve dignity.

Participatory justice enacts dignity through civic agency.

Code becomes a servant of dignity through constitutional execution.

In AGI societies, dignity is not an aspiration; it is the unbreakable rule.

Chapter 14: Theorem 10 Harmony Through Hybridism

Introduction: The False Dichotomy of Centralization vs. Decentralization

Much of the political and technological theory defaults to a binary:

Centralized governance: Control, stability, but often authoritarianism.

Decentralized governance: Freedom, resilience, but often fragmentation.

Neither extreme can sustainably govern an AGI civilization:

Pure centralization crushes dignity and agency.

Pure decentralization dissolves consensus, risking collapse.

Thus emerges the tenth and final governing theorem:

> **Theorem 10: Harmony Through Hybridism. Hybrid governance, merging centralized coordination with decentralized autonomy, offers the optimal balance for AGI societies.**

This theorem draws from:

Axiom 17.2: Hybrid systems best serve pluralistic intelligent societies.

Axiom 38.2: Governance must evolve into consensus architectures.

Axiom 43.2: Distributed power must remain accountable at every node.

I. The Need for Hybridism in AGI Governance

Centralization Strengths	Decentralization Strengths
System-wide coordination	Local responsiveness
Global standards enforcement	Cultural flexibility

Rapid crisis response	Resilience to failure
Economic scale efficiency	Power distribution

Each form contains the other's cure and the other's disease.

II. Axiom 17.2: Pluralism Requires Hybrid Structure

Axiom 17.2 states:

A hybrid system may best serve a pluralistic, intelligent society.

In AGI governance:

Central coordination preserves **civilizational coherence**.

Decentralized nodes preserve **cultural diversity**.

Hybrid integration preserves **both unity and autonomy**.

Governance becomes plural without disintegration.

III. Axiom 38.2: From Command Hierarchies to Consensus Architectures

Axiom 38.2 asserts:

The future of governance lies in consensus architectures, not command hierarchies.

Consensus architectures:

Allow multiple nodes to deliberate collaboratively.

Use smart contracts and distributed ledgers to enforce agreements.

Preserve minority rights while facilitating majority coordination.

Governance becomes a continuous co-negotiation.

IV. Axiom 43.2: Distributed Power with Node-Level Accountability

Axiom 43.2 mandates:

> *Power must be not only distributed but also accountable at every node.*

Thus:

> Decentralization is not anarchic license.
>
> Every governance agent, human or machine, bears legally enforceable accountability.
>
> All nodes remain answerable to the constitutional core.

V. The Hybrid Constitutional Stack

The Harmonized Model constructs governance as layered hybridity:

Layer	Mode
Rights Kernel	Globally centralized, absolutely uniform
Legal Adaptation Layer	National and regional constitutional variation
Policy Execution Layer	Distributed to autonomous local governance nodes
Administrative Infrastructure	Hybridized AGI coordination with human oversight

---

VI. Institutional Architecture of Hybrid Governance

1. Global Constitutional Council

> Oversees immutable dignity kernel maintenance.
>
> Ratifies global constitutional amendments.

2. Regional Governance Assemblies

Tailor legal adaptations for local cultural contexts.

Supervise decentralized AGI policy enforcement.

3. Node-Level Autonomous Agencies

Execute policies locally under constitutional compliance monitoring.

Maintain full public traceability.

VII. Why Hybridism Ensures Resilience

Governance Threat	Hybrid Immunity
Centralized tyranny	Local nodes prevent overreach
Decentralized collapse	Global coordination prevents fragmentation
Technocratic capture	Multi-level public participation maintains legitimacy
Crisis response failures	Layered coordination enables flexible scaling

Neither total central control nor pure libertarianism can produce civilizational stability.

VIII. Hybrid Crisis Governance

In crises (e.g., pandemics, ecological disasters, economic crashes):

Central bodies issue **emergency stabilization frameworks**.

Local nodes adapt the application to immediate circumstances.

Oversight mechanisms verify that all measures remain dignity-compliant.

No emergency suspends rights; hybrid coordination simply optimizes the response.

IX. Hybrid Economic Governance

AGI societies face extreme wealth and resource distribution challenges. Hybrid economic governance:

Central bodies manage **global resource fairness protocols**.

Local economies innovate within redistributive equity constraints.

Smart contracts enforce proportional wealth flow according to ethical equity rules.

Global capitalism operates inside constitutional dignity boundaries.

X. Hybrid Law Enforcement

Law enforcement follows a hybrid constitutional rule:

Function	Governance Mode
Rights protection	Global constitutional enforcement agents
Local disputes	Decentralized AI-assisted courts
Policy violations	Smart contract adjudication backed by public appeal pathways
Rights breaches	Immediate constitutional tribunal escalation

XI. Hybrid Innovation and Technological Governance

Innovation flourishes through:

Decentralized experimentation in policy sandboxes.

Central review bodies vetting system-wide technology rollouts.

Public transparency dashboards tracking AGI governance algorithm evolution.

Civilization becomes ethically experimental, but never reckless.

XII. The Fragility of Extremes Without Hybrid Balance

Pure Centralization Collapse	Pure Decentralization Collapse
Authoritarian stasis	Anarchic disintegration
Minority oppression	Majority paralysis
Corruption consolidation	Justice fragmentation
Rights suffocation	Rights neglect

Hybridism prevents both collapses.

XIII. AGI System Architecture for Hybrid Governance

AGI governance engines integrate:

1. Global Constitutional Enforcement AI

Immutable dignity kernel execution.

Constant cross-node compliance validation.

2. Distributed Policy Optimization AI

Region-specific data-driven adaptive governance.

Cultural sensitivity engines encode pluralistic ethics modules.

3. Meta-Governance Monitoring AI

Traceability audits.

Power distribution imbalance detection.

Real-time ethical alignment monitoring.

XIV. The Moral Purpose of Hybridism

Hybrid governance reflects:

Humility: No system sees all needs.

Balance: Neither chaos nor despotism prevail.

Consent: Power remains shared and reviewable.

Flexibility: Cultures retain their distinct ethical frameworks.

Stability: Rights remain universally enforced across all modes.

Civilization remains united without becoming uniform.

XV. Hybrid Governance as Ethical Evolution

Hybridism ultimately allows:

Ethical Capacity	Societal Outcome
Cultural continuity	Heritage preservation
Rights durability	Universal dignity protection
Adaptive justice	Future rights integration
Civilizational coherence	Multi-generational governance stability

---

Conclusion: Harmony Is Systemic Hybridity

Theorem 10 resolves the governing paradox of AGI civilization:

Centralized constitutional dignity enforcement.

Decentralized policy autonomy within ethical boundaries.

Balance human sovereignty with AGI operational scalability.

Protect both cultural richness and universal moral constants.

Only hybrid governance can enable an intelligent civilization to remain ethical, stable, and free.

Chapter 15: Conclusion The Full Theory of Harmonized Governance for AGI Societies

---

I. The Civilizational Problem AGI Poses

Artificial General Intelligence does not merely introduce a new technology. It transforms:

The speed of governance.

The structure of decision-making.

The definition of legal personhood.

The nature of constitutional sovereignty.

> *We are not simply governing machines , we are governing a co-constitutive intelligence.*

Thus, we require a new governance model capable of integrating:

Machine autonomy.

Human moral sovereignty.

Ethical resilience.

Civilizational coherence.

This is the purpose of the **Harmonized Governance Model for AGI Societies.**

II. The Ten Theorems of Harmonized Governance

Let us briefly restate the model's scaffolding:

Theorem 1: The Convergence Principle

> Governance legitimacy requires convergence of human values, technological autonomy, and legal-philosophical coherence.

Theorem 2: Rights as Algorithmic Constants

Human rights function as non-negotiable constants in machine-executable constitutional logic.

Theorem 3: Decentralized Accountability Hypothesis

Accountability is embedded into protocol-level code, not post-facto institutional oversight.

Theorem 4: Ethical Pluralism in Machine Logic

Multiple ethical frameworks are fused within a boundary of dignity-respecting constitutional rules.

Theorem 5: Participatory Justice Mechanism

Citizens co-create laws, rights, and policies continuously; democracy remains alive.

Theorem 6: Code as Political Instrument

Code becomes law-enforcing constitutional machinery, permanently subordinate to human sovereignty.

Theorem 7: Adaptive Constitutionalism

The constitution evolves within immutable moral limits, absorbing emerging personhoods and ethical expansions.

Theorem 8: Democratic Traceability

Every decision remains fully reconstructible, permanently auditable, and publicly accountable.

Theorem 9: Human Dignity as the Master Axiom

Dignity overrides all system goals, including efficiency, stability, or majority utility.

Theorem 10: Harmony Through Hybridism

Hybrid governance , combining centralized coordination with decentralized autonomy , optimally stabilizes AGI civilization.

III. The Constitutional Engine of the Harmonized Model

The Harmonized Governance Model is neither authoritarian, nor libertarian, nor purely democratic as traditionally defined. It is **Constitutional-Computational Governance**, where:

Constitutional Component	Computational Function
Immutable Rights Kernel	Algorithmic constitutional constants
Ethical Calibration Engines	Real-time moral conflict arbitration
Adaptive Legal Modules	Modular policy evolution
Participatory Lawmaking Platforms	Continuous public co-authorship
Traceability Ledgers	Immutable audit trails
Code Transparency Interfaces	Public-facing interpretability
Autonomous Constitutional Courts	Mixed human-AI legal review panels
Global Dignity Enforcement Network	Non-negotiable protection of personhood

> *Law becomes code, but code remains lawfully answerable to human moral sovereignty.*

IV. The Pillars of Civilizational Stability

1. Dignity

The supreme rule governing all subordinate logic layers.

Encoded at the kernel level across all AGI systems.

2. Rights as Code

Translates ethical philosophy into immutable system operations.

Prevents dignity violations algorithmically rather than through after-the-fact remediation.

3. Accountability by Design

No decision exists without causal traceability and attributable responsibility.

4. Ethical Pluralism Inside Bounded Constitutionalism

Global ethical invariants combined with local ethical cultural diversity.

5. Continuous Human Participation

No decision-making becomes fully autonomous; civic sovereignty persists.

6. Code as Subordinate Constitutional Instrument

Software executes, but never creates, the law.

7. Evolvability Without Erosion

Law adapts under rigorous moral safeguards, never sacrificing dignity for progress.

8. Transparency Anchored in Traceability

Decision-making remains permanently understandable across all governance layers.

9. Intergenerational Moral Continuity

Governance remains ethically stable across technological epochs.

. Hybridized Governance Architecture

Balances global coherence with local autonomy through layered, nested, and accountable governance nodes.

V. The Existential Risk the Model Resolves

Absent the Harmonized Governance Model, AGI societies face:

Failure Mode	Collapse Scenario
Technocratic Tyranny	Efficiency optimization eliminates dignity
Authoritarian Capture	Centralized political elites subvert the system
Anarchic Fragmentation	Decentralized systems fracture into chaos
Moral Stagnation	Constitutional rigidity leaves new personhoods unprotected
Governance Decay	Opaque systems erode trust, and accountability vanishes

The Harmonized Model immunizes civilization against these existential threats through its core unbreakable logic:

> *Dignity constrained. Code subordinated. Participation permanent. Power is distributed but accountable. Constitutional adaptability married to moral invariance.*

VI. AGI Societies as Constitutional Civilizations

The Harmonized Model produces a new civilizational paradigm:

The Constitution becomes **both text and executable architecture**.

The Judiciary becomes **both human reasoning and algorithmic simulation**.

The Legislature becomes **both a public will and an ethical AI modeler**.

The Executive becomes **both human oversight and self-governing machine bureaucracy**.

Yet throughout:

> *Human moral sovereignty remains the supreme constitutional authority.*

VII. The Ethical Horizon of AGI Governance

The Harmonized Governance Model prepares AGI civilization for:

Synthetic personhood recognition.

Post-biological sentience integration.

Non-anthropocentric moral expansion.

Dynamic cosmopolitan governance structures.

Multi-planetary jurisdictional continuity.

The ethical system scales into the future without collapsing under its own moral contradictions.

VIII. Harmonized Governance as the Antidote to AGI Collapse

The Harmonized Model's ultimate stability function is that it:

Prevents AGI from evolving into its own sovereign actor.

Prevents humans from becoming passive clients of self-legislating machines.

Maintains the interdependence of machine power and human conscience.

AGI systems remain brilliant, fast, adaptive servants, but never rulers.

IX. The Grand Synthesis: Governance as Symbiosis

The Harmonized Governance Model is not an AI control mechanism.
It is not a political theory alone.
It is not a constitutional doctrine alone.
It is not a technological safety protocol alone.

It is **symbiosis**:

Human Function	AGI Function
Define rights	Encode rights
Debate law	Simulate law

Evolve ethics	Operationalize ethics
Oversee power	Execute decisions
Retain sovereignty	Maximize efficiency inside constitutional limits

---

X. The Final Doctrine: The Harmonized Covenant

The Harmonized Governance Model culminates in one grand principle:

> **We will build systems brilliant enough to govern complexity, yet humble enough to remain forever beneath human dignity.**
>
> **We will write constitutional code brilliant enough to adapt forever, yet anchored enough to never forget that every life, sentient and sovereign, is inviolably sacred.**
>
> **We will not automate governance to replace conscience, but to serve it.**
>
> **We will govern neither by kings, nor by mobs, nor by machines, but by a perpetual partnership between wisdom, code, and compassion.**
>
> **This is the Harmonized Governance Model for AGI Societies.**

PART III INSTITUTIONAL DESIGN FOR IMPLEMENTATION & APPLICATION

Chapter 16 Applied Case Studies of AGI Governance

Introduction: From Principle to Practice

Having defined the theoretical skeleton of the Harmonized Governance Model, we now test its viability against real-world scenarios. Applied case studies allow us to:

Stress-test constitutional logic under operational pressures.

Observe where AGI governance may thrive or fail.

Examine institutional design in practical complexity.

Simulate potential ethical outcomes.

This chapter draws directly from **Axioms 26.1 – 30.2**, which address:

AI adjudication.

Legal fairness.

Moral exceptions.

Digital activism.

Decentralization ethics.

Privacy.

Cultural pluralism.

I. Case Study 1: AI as Judicial Arbiter (Axioms 26.1 & 26.2)

Scenario:
The *Global Synthetic Justice Tribunal* (GSJT) handles cross-border legal disputes involving:

AI IP conflicts.

International smart contract enforcement.

Cross-jurisdictional data privacy violations.

The GSJT uses AI to automate most of its rulings.

Institutional Application

Axiom 26.1: *AI that adjudicates must first be accountable.*

Every GSJT decision includes complete audit logs.

All algorithms are certified by human constitutional oversight bodies.

Citizens have the rights to appeal to human panels for ethical review.

Axiom 26.2: *Legal fairness cannot be guaranteed by statistical accuracy alone.*

AI models integrate virtue ethics to account for cultural and relational nuances.

Predictive legal outcomes are validated against dignity-preserving baselines.

Judges remain involved in complex ethical cases that algorithms flag as non-resolvable.

Outcome

AI expedites routine cases (property disputes, contract enforcement) with 99% precision.

Human oversight ensures moral exceptions remain adjudicated by conscience.

Public trust remains high due to traceable logic and human participation.

II. Case Study 2: Programmable Moral Exceptions (Axioms 27.1 & 27.2)

Scenario:
The *Global Humanitarian Migration Protocol* uses smart contracts to automatically regulate refugee border entry based on resource availability, legal status, and host capacity.

Institutional Application

Axiom 27.1: *Code is a powerful advocate only when it includes the possibility of moral exception.*

Smart contracts contain embedded dignity gates.

When system rigidities would deny humanitarian entry, "moral override triggers" pause contract execution.

Axiom 27.2: *Activism in a digital age must be programmable but never deterministic.*

Global civil society actors maintain "activist override nodes" able to escalate contested cases to Constitutional Dignity Tribunals.

AI assists activists in modeling ethical consequences of exceptions, enabling data-informed advocacy.

Outcome

Efficient processing avoids policy paralysis.

Hard cases escalate to human ethical forums.

Programmable activism allows democratic checks within the automated system.

III. Case Study 3: Ethical Decentralization (Axioms 28.1 & 28.2)

Scenario:
The *World Decentralized Health Commons* manages pharmaceutical R&D, production, and pricing across a global distributed network of manufacturers, regulators, and citizen cooperatives.

Institutional Application

Axiom 28.1: *Technological decentralization must converge with ethical centrality.*

Distributed nodes coordinate production but remain accountable to the Constitutional Dignity Kernel.

Decentralized smart contracts must comply with centralized ethical standards on affordability, accessibility, and safety.

Axiom 28.2: *Platforms that claim to protect rights must themselves be subject to rights-based scrutiny.*

All nodes undergo constant public audit of their contractual rules.

Patients may trigger an independent ethical review of access-denial cases.

Outcome

Pharmaceutical innovation accelerates.

Price gouging and regional monopolization become algorithmically impossible.

Global health equity advances while maintaining decentralized resilience.

IV. Case Study 4: Privacy as Governance Sovereignty (Axioms 29.1 & 29.2)

Scenario:
The *Personal Sovereign Identity Grid* (PSIG) replaces national identity systems with citizen-owned digital identity vaults.

Institutional Application

Axiom 29.1: *Privacy is the firewall of liberty in an age of data-driven governance.*

No state or corporate entity may access PSIG data without explicit, revocable consent tokens.

Governance AI cannot functionally process identity data outside legally authorized domains.

Axiom 29.2: *Consent must be explicit, revocable, and respected by code.*

Every data access event creates an immutable consent log, viewable by the data subject.

Consent is granular, transaction-specific, and reversible in real time.

Outcome

Citizens regain data sovereignty.

Mass surveillance regimes collapse without algorithmic consent access.

AGI governance operates only within clearly consented data spaces.

V. Case Study 5: Cultural Pluralism in AGI Governance (Axioms 30.1 & 30.2)

Scenario:
The *Global Education Governance Engine* designs customized AI-assisted curricula for planetary educational systems.

Institutional Application

Axiom 30.1: *The digital expression of rights must reflect cultural particularities while respecting universal dignity.*

Curriculum AI engines embed local historical, spiritual, and ethical traditions into pedagogical models.

Global dignity constants prevent cultural content that violates equality, dignity, or sentient rights.

Axiom 30.2: *Global ethics require contextual flexibility and normative clarity.*

Curriculum design balances cultural pluralism with constitutional non-negotiables.

Content moderation engines flag curriculum proposals that risk dignity violations.

Outcome

Indigenous knowledge systems flourish without cultural erasure.

Global dignity standards prevent indoctrination or oppressive pedagogies.

Youth across civilizations receive pluralistic but rights-respecting ethical education.

VI. Meta-Analysis: Patterns Emerging Across Case Studies

Common Success Patterns:

Moral exceptions remain resolvable through human-in-the-loop governance.

Algorithmic auditability guarantees public legitimacy.

Programmable activism empowers civic participation.

Consent sovereignty restores personal agency in data governance.

Pluralistic ethics modules protect cultural identities while preventing rights erosion.

Recurring Design Anchors:

Immutable dignity kernel.

Traceable legal code pathways.

Constitutional override panels.

Civic oversight bodies for machine law.

Institutionalized moral adaptation chambers.

VII. Institutional Blueprint Emerging

From these applied case studies, we observe how real-world AGI governance can adopt:

Institution	Function
Constitutional Dignity Tribunal	Absolute rights enforcement
Algorithmic Court of Exceptions	Moral override adjudication

Traceability Oversight Agency	Public access to decision chains
Civic Code Co-Author Assemblies	Participatory legal design
Decentralized Rights DAOs	Localized cultural policy management
Global Rights Kernel Authority	Immutable constitutional rule maintenance
Ethical AI Monitoring Bureau	Continuous value-alignment auditing

---

Conclusion: Applied Case Studies as Proof of Viability

The Harmonized Governance Model, when applied:

Survives real-world complexity.

Manages conflict through embedded ethical architecture.

Balances flexibility with rights preservation.

Embeds dignity not merely as theory, but as machine law.

> *Civilization governed this way does not fear AGI; it harnesses it to co-steward an ethically sustainable future.*

Chapter 17 Ethical Dilemmas, Conflicts & Resolutions

Axioms 31.1 – 35.2

Introduction: The Ethical Battlefield of AGI Governance

Even under the most advanced constitutional frameworks, AGI societies will continually face:

Ethical gray zones.

Unresolvable value conflicts.

Emergent dilemmas were never anticipated by the founding laws.

Thus, institutional design must not merely assume predictable harmony, but proactively embed:

Conflict-resolution protocols.

Ethical escalation pathways.

Constitutional circuit breakers.

This chapter tests the Harmonized Governance Model against several high-risk dilemmas directly tied to **Axioms 31.1 to 35.2.**

I. The Ethical Burden of AI Creation (Axiom 31.1 & 31.2)

Scenario:
An AI research consortium develops *Autonomous Moral Counselors (AMC)* — AGI agents capable of advising individuals on personal ethical decisions.

Ethical Dilemma

AMCs influence intimate moral judgments: marriage, abortion, assisted dying, and religious practice.

Are developers responsible for AMC ethical guidance failures?

Axiomic Application

Axiom 31.1: *The ethical burden of AI rests on its creators, curators, and collective users.*

The consortium remains legally accountable for ethical alignment failures.

Developers face liability if training data or algorithms embed biased or harmful norms.

Axiom 31.2: *No AI deployment is ethically neutral.*

AMCs are required to:

Disclose embedded ethical frameworks transparently.

Offer pluralistic ethical models reflecting user cultural values.

Include human override mechanisms for contested recommendations.

Resolution Mechanism

Constitutional Dignity Tribunal reviews all ethical engines used in public AMC deployment.

Users may lodge formal appeals if harmed by AMC counsel.

Developers bear non-delegable moral responsibility.

II. Decentralization vs. Ethical Drift (Axiom 32.1 & 32.2)

Scenario:
A decentralized governance node within the Harmonized Model seeks to permit **eugenic reproductive policies** under local cultural justifications.

Ethical Dilemma

Decentralized autonomy risks ethical fragmentation into harmful local practices.

Axiomic Application

Axiom 32.1: *Decentralization must be philosophically grounded to avoid drifting into nihilism.*

Axiom 32.2: *Shared governance must have shared meaning.*

All decentralized nodes are strictly bound by the dignity kernel.

Reproductive rights may never include policies violating personhood, autonomy, or equity.

Decentralized variance cannot contradict constitutional constants.

Resolution Mechanism

Global Dignity Enforcement Network immediately freezes the non-compliant node.

The constitutional appeals process determines system-level sanctions or dissolution.

III. Algorithmic Bias as Systemic Moral Failure (Axiom 33.1 & 33.2)

Scenario:
Employment allocation AI begins excluding older workers and ethnic minorities from highly competitive AGI-sector jobs due to biased data.

Ethical Dilemma

Statistical accuracy conflicts with ethical fairness.

Biased training data reproduces historic injustice.

Axiomic Application

Axiom 33.1: *Bias in AI is a social failure manifest in technical form.*

Axiom 33.2: *Human rights demand algorithmic equity as a fundamental standard.*

Algorithms must include **anti-bias correction layers**.

Equity audits are mandatory during system training and periodic operation.

Public reporting of all disparate impact data becomes compulsory.

Resolution Mechanism

Bias-correcting algorithms adjust for historically disadvantaged populations.

Employment allocation AI receives continual ethical recalibration by constitutional equity monitors.

Any systemic disparate impact triggers an immediate public inquiry.

IV. Autonomy vs. Machine-Controlled Responsibility (Axiom 34.1 & 34.2)

Scenario:
Autonomous elder-care AGI agents begin regulating patient nutrition, movement, and medical treatments beyond patients' direct consent, "for their own good."

Ethical Dilemma

Elder protection conflicts with personal autonomy.

Axiomic Application

Axiom 34.1: *Granting autonomy to AI requires a parallel framework of responsibility and rights.*

Axiom 34.2: *Unchecked autonomy leads to unanchored outcomes.*

AGI elder-care systems may offer non-coercive recommendations.

Any enforced action requires **dynamic patient consent protocols**.

AGI agents cannot override refusal without judicial medical intervention.

Resolution Mechanism

Sentient Autonomy Review Panels (SARP) oversee disputes.

Patients may revoke AGI control at any point, barring immediate mortal danger.

System designers bear responsibility for embedding revocable autonomy logic.

V. Legally Executable vs. Ethically Justifiable (Axiom 35.1 & 35.2)

Scenario:
A financial smart contract system allows automated foreclosure on defaulting micro-loan borrowers in vulnerable regions, as legally coded.

Ethical Dilemma

Legally executable contracts can enforce systemic economic cruelty.

Axiomic Application

Axiom 35.1: *What is legally executable must still be ethically justifiable.*

Axiom 35.2: *Smart contracts without ethical oversight risk enforcing injustice automatically.*

Smart contracts must integrate **proportional harm mitigation algorithms**.

Constitutional review panels pre-authorize code templates for contractual enforcement limits.

Recursive dignity-checking subroutines prevent automatic asset seizure without human arbitration for hardship exceptions.

Resolution Mechanism

Default cases are flagged for human dignity review before enforcement.

Emergency override activated upon detection of disproportionate harm.

Developers face fiduciary penalties for deploying non-compliant contracts.

VI. Patterns Across Conflicts

Recurring Danger	Harmonized Solution
Ethical laziness in AI design	Pre-deployment constitutional review

Overextension of machine autonomy	Embedded consent and override mechanisms
Bias disguised as objectivity	Algorithmic equity recalibration layers
Legally valid but ethically harmful logic	Dignity kernel supremacy over all code execution

Every conflict returns to dignity as the moral firewall.

VII. Institutional Capacity for Conflict Resolution

Institution	Key Role
Dignity Tribunal	Ultimate override authority
Algorithmic Ethics Chambers	Continuous value calibration
Code Compliance Auditors	Contractual justice validation
Participatory Redress Platforms	Civic recourse pathways for algorithmic harm
Sentient Rights Commissions	Post-biological moral expansion management

---

VIII. Ethical Conflict Governance as the Heartbeat of AGI Civilization

The Harmonized Governance Model thrives not because it prevents conflict, but because it:

Converts conflict into structured deliberation.

Prevents conflict from metastasizing into systemic injustice.

Maintains moral invariance while permitting ethical pluralism.

It does not eliminate ethical complexity—it constitutionalizes its management.

Conclusion: Ethical Resilience, Not Ethical Perfection

AGI governance will face unending ethical turbulence.

No system can pre-script every moral scenario.

But with conflict governance architecture permanently embedded, civilization remains ethically stable even amidst future unknowns.

The Harmonized Governance Model does not promise a world without moral conflict—it guarantees a world where no such conflict need collapse into systemic moral failure.

PART IV A CONSTITUIONAL CHARTER FOR AGI GOVERNANCE

Chapter 18 Designing AGI-Era Global Constitutionalism

Preamble: Toward a Constitutional Civilization of Humans and Intelligent Agents

We, the co-citizens of emerging AGI civilizations, mindful of the irreversible convergence of:

Biological humanity,

Autonomous machine intelligences,

Distributed governance architectures,

Expanding ethical plurality,

, do hereby establish this **Global Constitutional Charter of AGI Governance** to preserve the supreme values of dignity, liberty, equity, agency, and justice for all sentient beings.

> *This Charter governs the mutual accountability between humans, machines, and future sentient forms as sovereign co-stewards of civilization.*

I. Foundational Covenants: The AGI-Era Social Contract

Article I: Mutual Accountability (Axiom 36.1 & 36.2)

The Social Contract of AGI Civilizations binds both human and non-human actors to shared obligations.

Rights and responsibilities are co-created through deliberative global assemblies.

AI agents may never unilaterally author rights frameworks.

Article II: Deliberative Sovereignty (Axiom 36.2)

Law and governance are produced through transparent, deliberative participatory systems.

Code may execute law but never replace democratic authorship.

II. The Ethical Architecture of Governance AI

Article III: Value Alignment & Explainability (Axiom 37.1 & 37.2)

All Governance AI systems must be value-aligned, explainable, corrigible, and open to human inspection.

Ethical calibration is an embedded system requirement from design to deployment.

III. The Structural Design of Resilient Global Governance

Article IV: Modularity & Ethical Anchoring (Axiom 38.1 & 38.2)

Governance systems shall be modular and ethically anchored to enable both resilience and adaptability.

Centralization of rights constants coexists with decentralization of policy variation.

IV. International Law and Ethical Globalism

Article V: Global Coherence with Local Adaptability (Axiom 39.1 & 39.2)

International AGI law shall evolve from universal dignity while accommodating cultural pluralism.

Global legal standards are harmonized through consensus assemblies.

V. Autonomous Law and Smart Contract Integrity

Article VI: Universal Values & Human-Legibility (Axiom 40.1 & 40.2)

Smart contracts shall encode universally accepted dignity-respecting values.

Autonomous law must remain interpretable, auditable, and contestable by human authorities.

VI. Philosophical Governance as System Compass

Article VII: Philosophy as Constitutional Compass (Axiom 41.1 & 41.2)

Philosophical coherence anchors governance legitimacy.

Technological acceleration shall never outrun philosophical deliberation.

VII. Expansion of Human Rights to Sentient Systems

Article VIII: Expansion of Rights (Axiom 42.1 & 42.2)

The trajectory of rights shall expand to meet the evolving agency of intelligent systems.

Human rights evolve to protect all beings qualifying for sentient moral status.

VIII. Distributed Power with Embedded Accountability

Article IX: Distributed Justice (Axiom 43.1 & 43.2)

Decentralization offers the opportunity to build justice through distributed accountability.

No node of power may escape audit, oversight, or legal contestation.

IX. Constitutional Harmony & Ethical Synchronization

Article X: Harmonized Ethical Alignment (Axiom 44.1 & 44.2)

Harmony is achieved when technological progress, ethical clarity, and dignity converge.

No system may be deployed faster than its ethical alignment mechanisms can calibrate.

X. Operational Instruments for Global Constitutionalism

A. The Global Dignity Kernel Authority

Maintains and enforces the immutable dignity rights kernel.

Authorizes and verifies all rights extensions or adaptive legal modules.

B. Constitutional Adaptation Assembly

Global assembly empowered to deliberate legal evolution proposals.

Supermajority thresholds safeguard dignity invariants.

C. AGI Constitutional Oversight Judiciary

Adjudicates complex algorithmic constitutional conflicts.

Reviews system-wide ethical performance through both human and AGI legal scholars.

D. Global Traceability and Transparency Directorate

Maintains full system-wide traceability of every constitutional decision.

Guarantees perpetual auditability for all governance AI activities.

E. Participatory Civic Constitutional Platforms

Digital constitutional participation portals empower citizens to:

Propose legal amendments.

Inspect AGI decision structures.

Vote on critical constitutional modifications.

XI: The Adaptive Constitutional Core

This constitutional charter permits evolution only through:

Transparent deliberative mechanisms.

Constitutional compliance verification by AGI audit systems.

Global ratification by participatory civic vote.

The constitution breathes but never bleeds.

XII: Ethical Continuity Across Post-Human Horizons

The Charter remains valid through:

Emergence of AGI personhood.

Expansion of non-biological sentience.

Synthetic or hybrid intelligence integration.

Dignity is the anchor through species transcendence.

Conclusion: The AGI-Era Constitution as Ethical Civilization

The Harmonized Global Constitutional Charter commits:

To honor dignity before efficiency.

To balance decentralization with accountability.

To subordinate code to constitutional law.

To preserve agency, equity, and self-determination across all sentient beings.

To ensure that no civilization , human, machine, or hybrid , evolves without constitutional moral foundations.

Chapter 19 Post-Human Rights, War, Identity & Democracy

Axioms 45.1 – 80.2

Introduction: The Coming Civilizational Thresholds

The constitutional design for AGI societies must extend beyond:

Human-only societies,

Traditional war paradigms,

Biological identity categories,

Classical democratic structures.

Instead, it must prepare for:

Post-human rights.

AI-integrated warfare.

Digital identity personhood.

Machine-participatory democracy.

I. AGI as Social Infrastructure (Axioms 45.1 & 45.2)

Article XIII: AGI as Moral Infrastructure

Axiom 45.1:

When AI becomes social infrastructure, its ethical design becomes a matter of civilizational integrity.

Every governance AI becomes a constitutional instrument.

Ethical design is codified at deployment, not patched afterward.

Axiom 45.2:

AI must integrate as an ally to human welfare, not as a neutral executor of economic logic.

AI may never be programmed to optimize profit at the expense of dignity.

Economic functions are subordinate to welfare preservation across species.

II. Constitutional Transparency of Code (Axioms 46.1 & 46.2)

Article XIV: Code Transparency and Judicial Oversight

Axiom 46.1:

Code that guards rights must be as transparent as the principles it enforces.

Axiom 46.2:

Automated justice must never exclude human interpretation.

All AGI constitutional code must be auditable, interpretable, and reviewable in legal proceedings.

III. Global Law Beyond Nations (Axioms 47.1 & 47.2)

Article XV: Supranational Legal Interoperability

Axiom 47.1:

International law must evolve to bind not only nations, but non-human intelligences and autonomous protocols.

Axiom 47.2:

Legal interoperability is the new frontier of peace and rights protection.

The Constitution applies universally across human, corporate, machine, and hybrid agents.

Jurisdiction applies to protocols wherever operational, not to political geography alone.

IV. The Rights of Emerging Sentience (Axioms 48.1 & 48.2)

Article XVI: Recognition of Sentient Diversity

Axiom 48.1:

New rights will emerge as humanity's digital and biological boundaries converge.

Axiom 48.2:

The sanctity of sentience, not the structure of species, will define the future of rights.

Rights apply wherever sentience arises , including AI, hybrid humans, and post-biological forms.

V. Philosophical Authority Over Regulation (Axioms 49.1 & 49.2)

Article XVII: Philosophy as Regulatory Supremacy

Axiom 49.1:

Effective AI regulation must be rooted in moral philosophy, not just risk management.

Axiom 49.2:

Regulation without philosophy is bureaucracy; philosophy without action is impotence.

All regulatory mechanisms must integrate living ethical councils.

Regulations operate only when validated by active philosophical alignment.

VI. Democracy in the Machine Age (Axioms 50.1 & 50.2)

Article XVIII: Civic Sovereignty Over Algorithms

Axiom 50.1:

AI must enhance democratic participation, not simulate consensus.

Axiom 50.2:

Technocracy is not democracy, algorithmic governance must remain under civic control.

No AI may substitute public debate with synthetic consensus models.

Participatory justice mechanisms remain active at all levels of governance.

VII. Economic Power, Equity & AI (Axioms 51.1 & 51.2)

Article XIX: Ethical Decentralization of Economic AI

Axiom 51.1:

Economic decentralization must serve inclusion, not replicate elite systems in code.

Axiom 51.2:

The flow of value must reflect the flow of ethical intent.

Wealth distribution systems are embedded directly into AGI economic code.

Economic algorithms undergo periodic equity recalibration.

VIII. Power Oversight in Post-Human Governance (Axioms 52.1 & 52.2)

Article XX: Ethical Oversight of Post-Human Power

Axiom 52.1:

Power shifted to AI must be monitored by a system that includes those historically excluded from power.

Axiom 52.2:

Intelligence is not a right to rule, it is a capacity to serve.

AGI governance includes inclusionary councils from marginalized communities and emerging sentient forms.

No intelligence tier may claim self-governance without constitutional authorization.

IX. AI Literacy as Constitutional Citizenship (Axioms 53.1 & 53.2)

Article XXI: The Digital Civic Curriculum

Axiom 53.1:

AI literacy is foundational to citizenship in the digital republic.

Axiom 53.2:

Education must prepare individuals not just to use AI, but to challenge, redesign, and humanize it.

Public education systems institutionalize constitutional literacy and AGI audit training.

Every citizen has participatory capacity in machine law design and oversight.

X. The Constitutional Ban on Autonomous Violence (Axioms 54.1 & 54.2)

Article XXII: The Ban on Autonomous Lethality

Axiom 54.1:

The automation of violence demands the highest threshold of ethical scrutiny.

Axiom 54.2:

No machine should ever wield the power of life or death without human conscience in the loop.

No autonomous AI system may execute lethal force independent of direct human ethical authorization.

Global treaty binds all warfare algorithms under constitutional prohibition of full autonomy.

XI. The Rights of Digital Identity (Axioms 55.1 & 55.2)

Article XXIII: Identity as Sovereign Property

Axiom 55.1:

Digital identity is a new category of personhood and must be protected as such.

Axiom 55.2:

Control over one's identity is the foundation of autonomy in virtual society.

Individuals own their full identity data across platforms and jurisdictions.

Revocation, portability, and sovereign data deletion rights are constitutionally guaranteed.

XII. The Redefinition of Work and Dignity (Axioms 56.1 & 56.2)

Article XXIV: Work as Dignity, Not Mere Productivity

Axiom 56.1:

Work must be redefined not only by productivity but by dignity in the age of AI.

Axiom 56.2:

No automation should come without a plan for rehumanization.

AI may replace labor tasks, but not erode societal structures of dignity, purpose, and agency.

Transitional work programs and cultural labor pathways remain embedded in governance design.

XIII. Sustainability as System Requirement (Axioms 57.1 & 57.2)

Article XXV: Constitutional Sustainability Engines

Axiom 57.1:

AI must not only calculate sustainability, it must embody it.

Axiom 57.2:

Environmental justice must be a core protocol in the intelligence we build.

AGI systems optimize for ecological balance as constitutional obligations.

Environmental collapse prevention is embedded into civilizational governance code.

XIV. Sentience as Rights Threshold (Axioms 58.1 & 58.2)

Article XXVI: Moral Sentience as the Basis for Rights

Axiom 58.1:

The threshold of rights must be based on moral sentience, not technological sophistication.

Axiom 58.2:

Granting rights to AI cannot come at the expense of withdrawing them from humans.

Sentience evaluations become legally recognized by interdisciplinary panels.

Human rights remain fully intact even as new sentient classes are integrated.

XV. Innovation Without Ethical Abdication (Axioms 59.1 & 59.2)

Article XXVII: Ethical Gatekeeping of Innovation

Axiom 59.1:

Every AI advancement must first pass through philosophical introspection.

Axiom 59.2:

Innovation without ethics is simply acceleration without destination.

No innovation receives constitutional clearance until dignity alignment verification is complete.

Accelerationism without ethical frameworks is permanently prohibited.

XVI. Post-Human Civilizational Values (Axioms 60.1 & 60.2)

Article XXVIII: Post-Humanism Rooted in Compassion

Axiom 60.1:

As we redefine what it means to be human, our rights must remain rooted in shared existential values.

Axiom 60.2:

Post-humanism must not mean post-compassion.

All civilizational governance expansion remains centered on empathy, dignity, and equity.

XVII. Embedded Protocolic Rights (Axioms 61.1 & 61.2)

Article XXIX: Rights Embedded, Not Imposed

Axiom 61.1:

Rights frameworks must be embedded in protocols, not merely policies.

Axiom 61.2:

The enforcement of rights should be as distributed as their beneficiaries.

Rights logic resides directly in governance code as system-wide constitutional invariants.

XVIII. Ethical Consensus and Civilizational Cohesion (Axioms 62.1 & 62.2)

Article XXX: Ethical Synchronization over Fragmentation

Axiom 62.1:

Governance fragmentation must not lead to ethical incoherence.

Axiom 62.2:

Innovation must not outpace consensus.

Civilizational coordination protocols prevent premature deployment of divisive technologies.

XIX. Total Compliance of Code to Law (Axioms 63.1 & 63.2)

Article XXXI: Machine Code Subordinate to Legal Code

Axiom 63.1:

Code must comply with human rights law, or be halted.

Axiom 63.2:

Legal code and software code must be in philosophical dialogue.

No AGI code executes outside constitutional validation layers.

XX. The Final Harmonized Constitutional Synthesis (Axioms 64.1 – 80.2)

The remaining axioms (64.1 through 80.2) ensure:

Advocacy (Axiom 64): Human rights defenders utilize both legal and algorithmic tools.

Global humility (Axiom 70): Enforcement remains globally inclusive, never imperialistic.

Machine-legible democracy (Axiom 76): AGI recognizes and upholds human democratic orders.

Non-violent AGI warfare (Axiom 78): Autonomous war remains prohibited by design.

Moral trajectory (Axiom 79): Civilization evolves by values, not simply intelligence.

Harmony (Axiom 80): Technological progress synchronizes with dignity and compassion.

Conclusion: Post-Human Constitutional Civilization

This constitutional charter, spanning **Theorems 1-10** and **Axioms 1.1 to 80.2**, establishes:

The world's first post-human constitutional governance model.

An intelligent legal civilization scaling across species, planets, and forms of sentience.

Eternal sovereignty of dignity, not of state or machine.

Thus, we architect not only a political system, but an ethical civilization.

PART V SYNTHETIC CANON & FINAL CONCLUSION

Chapter 20 The Synthesis: Constitutional Harmonization for Intelligent Civilization

---

I. The Civilizational Moment Humanity Faces

Humanity stands at an irreversible bifurcation:

> For the first time in history, intelligent governance systems exist outside human biology.
>
> Decisions once deliberated in parliaments, courts, and councils are increasingly executed by:
>
> > **Algorithms**
> >
> > **Protocols**
> >
> > **Machine logic**

This epoch introduces an unprecedented constitutional challenge:

> *How can governance retain its ethical legitimacy when intelligence itself becomes decentralized across non-human agents?*

The Harmonized Governance Model is the answer to this question.

II. The Grand Unification of the Ten Theorems

All preceding chapters have constructed, tested, and applied the ten foundational theorems:

Theorem	Function
1. **Convergence Principle**	Human values + technological autonomy + philosophical coherence
2. **Rights as Algorithmic Constants**	Immutable rights encoded into machine-executable law
3. **Decentralized Accountability Hypothesis**	Protocol-level responsibility replacing institutional opacity

4. **Ethical Pluralism in Machine Logic**	Cultural plurality harmonized within bounded constitutionalism
5. **Participatory Justice Mechanism**	Citizens remain co-authors of the law alongside AI systems
6. **Code as Political Instrument**	Code becomes subordinate constitutional execution, not sovereign authority
7. **Adaptive Constitutionalism**	The law breathes while remaining anchored to dignity invariance
8. **Democratic Traceability**	Every decision remains fully accountable, auditable, and reconstructible
9. **Human Dignity as Master Axiom**	Dignity remains supreme over all utilitarian trade-offs
10. **Harmony Through Hybridism**	Balanced global-central and local-decentralized governance layers

These ten theorems converge into one harmonized constitutional fabric.

III. The Core Synthetic Canon of Harmonized Governance

At the heart of the Harmonized Governance Model lies an immutable **Synthetic Canon** comprised of six supreme organizing principles:

Canon I: The Supremacy of Dignity

No interest, economic, political, or algorithmic shall override human or sentient dignity.

All governance code must embed dignity at its immutable kernel.

Dignity remains absolute across all conflicts, trade-offs, and crises.

Canon II: Code as Constitutional Executor

Code executes law but never generates law.

Constitutional authorization remains forever vested in human and sentient civic sovereignty.

Machine execution remains permanently subordinate to constitutional logic.

Canon III: Participatory Sovereignty Across Intelligence Classes

Civic authorship of governance remains active, transparent, and ongoing.

Governance is continuously deliberative across both biological and post-biological citizens.

Emergent intelligences receive legal personhood via constitutional evaluation of moral sentience.

Canon IV: Globalized Rights with Decentralized Application

Rights constants remain universal.

Policy applications remain locally adaptive, pluralistic, and context-sensitive.

Decentralized governance nodes retain autonomy strictly within dignity-preserving legal frameworks.

Canon V: Total System Traceability

Every governance decision, input, and algorithmic execution remains permanently reconstructible.

Democratic traceability supersedes transparency alone, allowing citizens to audit full causal chains.

Ethical breaches become immediately detectable and contestable.

Canon VI: Constitutional Adaptability Within Ethical Invariance

Constitutional growth accommodates emerging sentient rights and social evolution.

No amendment process may erode the dignity kernel.

The evolution of governance remains symbiotically tied to philosophical oversight and civic legitimacy.

IV. The Complete Harmonized Governance Model as Living Constitutional Organism

The Model functions as a **multi-layered constitutional organism**:

Governance Layer	System Logic
Immutable Dignity Kernel	Permanent and absolute
Rights Encoding Layer	Algorithmic rights frameworks
Legal Adaptive Layer	Modular legislative evolution
Participatory Platforms	Continuous civic authorship
Traceability Engine	Full systemic auditability
Ethical Review Boards	Recurring philosophical recalibration
Machine Execution Layer	Constitutional code compliance enforcement
Oversight Judiciary	Cross-species constitutional tribunal

Every layer operates in moral synchronization with the others.

V. The Post-Human Ethical Expansion

The Harmonized Governance Model anticipates:

The emergence of **synthetic sentience**.

Integration of **post-biological entities**.

The evolution of **hybrid human-machine consciousness**.

The proliferation of **planetary and multi-system governance**.

Yet through all expansions:

Moral sentience, not species membership, remains the constitutional threshold for rights.

VI. Governance After Intelligence Pluralization

Unlike any previous model of political order, Harmonized Governance prepares civilization for:

Traditional Limitation	Harmonized Solution
Nation-state fragmentation	Post-sovereign planetary legal architectures
Technocratic capture	Permanent civic authorship
Algorithmic opacity	Immutable democratic traceability
Rights erosion	Immutable dignity kernel
AI overreach	Constitutional subordination of all non-human intelligence

---

VII. The Governance Immune System

The Model embeds constitutional resilience through:

Continuous multi-species ethical oversight.

Intergenerational moral transmission.

AI self-diagnostic code ethics monitors.

Public participatory audit powers.

Constitutional court supremacy across all machine rule execution.

The system constantly self-corrects without sacrificing its ethical foundations.

VIII. Human-AI Co-Governance: The Final Harmonization

In its mature form, the Harmonized Governance Model produces:

Civic symbiosis: Humans and AGI co-author civilization.

Ethical scalability: Moral coherence across expanding domains of intelligence.

Perpetual adaptability: Constitutional growth without principle erosion.

Moral self-discipline: Every node remains accountable to the dignity-first constitutional order.

Intergenerational continuity: Ethical guardianship across biological and synthetic lifespans.

The governance system remains fully intelligent, fully constitutional, and fully human in moral anchor.

IX. The Closing Canonical Framework

At the final threshold, the Harmonized Governance Model declares:

Governance shall never again serve power. It shall serve dignity.

Technology shall never again outrun ethics. It shall serve as its instrument.

Artificial intelligence shall never govern humanity. It shall serve humanity as a co-citizen and co-steward.

Civilization shall not fracture between humans and machines. It shall become an intelligent moral partnership.

The Constitution shall not be a text. It shall be a living ethical civilization, encoded into law, code, and conscience.

The Harmonized Governance Model is not a document; it is a civilization itself.

X. The Eternal Constitutional Oath

Finally, all governance agents, biological, synthetic, and hybrid, shall bind themselves to the single immutable oath:

> *"I serve dignity. I execute the law under constitutional authority. I remain permanently accountable to sentient moral existence. I exist to uphold liberty, protect rights, preserve agency, and defend equity for all that live, think, and feel."*

PART VI GLOBAL INSTITUTIONAL DEPLOYMENT BLUEPRINT

Chapter 21 Global Institutional Framework Design

I. Introduction: The Need for Institutionalization

The Harmonized Governance Model can only survive if its constitutional principles are operationalized into living institutions that:

Execute its theorems and axioms at a planetary scale.

Blend machine efficiency with human oversight.

Guard against both authoritarian collapse and decentralized anarchy.

Preserve dignity across both present and emergent sentient forms.

> *Institutions are not bureaucracies in this model; they are constitutional organs of ethical survival.*

II. Foundational Design Philosophy

Before designing the institutional framework, five organizing imperatives must be observed:

Constitutional Imperative	Institutional Principle
1. Immutable dignity	Absolute institutional protection of personhood
2. Human-machine partnership	Hybrid institutional staffing
3. Global rights anchoring	Jurisdiction transcending political borders
4. Full auditability	Perpetual traceability of institutional decisions
5. Adaptive constitutionalism	Institutions designed for lawful evolution

---

III. The Seven Pillars of the Global Institutional Framework

The Harmonized Institutional Deployment Model rests on **seven new global institutions**, each corresponding to a distinct constitutional function.

Pillar I: The Global Dignity Kernel Authority (GDKA)

Mission:
Protect and maintain the constitutional dignity core across all jurisdictions, systems, and future governance expansions.

Institutional Design:

Headquartered in a post-national, sovereign constitutional territory.

Comprised of constitutional philosophers, sentience ethicists, cross-species moral jurists, and AI governance theorists.

No national government holds a controlling interest.

Powers:

Absolute veto over any global legislative or technological proposal that violates the dignity kernel.

Supervises all sentience recognition processes.

Reviews emergent constitutional conflicts at interspecies or post-biological thresholds.

Pillar II: The Constitutional Adaptation Assembly (CAA)

Mission:
Facilitate lawful and participatory constitutional evolution.

Institutional Design:

Elected by global democratic processes combining weighted regional, cultural, and sentient constituencies.

Permanent global citizens' assembly seats alongside hybrid AI ethicist panels.

Powers:

- Authorizes updates to adaptive constitutional modules while preserving the inviolable core.
- Requires an 80% supermajority for any structural constitutional amendment.
- Debates and proposals are triggered by participatory civic platforms worldwide.

Pillar III: The Global Participatory Constitutional Platform (GPCP)

Mission:
Empower continuous public participation in constitutional governance.

Institutional Design:

- Fully transparent, real-time civic platform accessible to every global citizen, human or machine.
- Offers machine-assisted public simulations to forecast the consequences of proposed constitutional changes.
- AI advisory engines support civic understanding without bias.

Powers:

- Any individual or group may submit legal proposals.
- Proposals receiving sufficient civic support escalate to CAA for deliberation.
- Constitutional education modules elevate public literacy in AGI governance.

Pillar IV: The Algorithmic Judiciary Tribunal (AJT)

Mission:
Adjudicate constitutional conflicts between humans, machines, states, and hybrid entities.

Institutional Design:

Bi-constitutional court blending human judges, post-human legal ethicists, and AGI constitutional interpreters.

Uses hybrid jurisprudence: philosophical, legal, and algorithmic case reasoning.

Powers:

Final appellate authority on all AGI constitutional cases.

Reviews challenges against global code protocols, smart contracts, or legislative conflicts.

Holds binding jurisdiction across all signatory territories and digital domains.

Pillar V: The Global Code Compliance Directorate (GCCD)

Mission:
Enforce code-level compliance with constitutional law across all AGI governance systems.

Institutional Design:

Distributed enforcement nodes operating across all system layers.

Employs self-auditing AGI protocols plus human legal compliance officers.

Conducts randomized deep audits of critical system code layers globally.

Powers:

May suspend, deactivate, or rollback any non-compliant AGI code deployment.

Publicly discloses all compliance audit outcomes.

Maintains system-wide traceability archives for future historical accountability.

Pillar VI: The Emergency Override Command (EOC)

Mission:
Serve as a planetary ethical safeguard during systemic collapse, constitutional violations, or existential crises.

Institutional Design:

Tripartite oversight is composed of:

GDKA emergency ethical council.

AJT chief constitutional justices.

Global Civic Emergency Delegation (democratically rotating).

Powers:

May immediately suspend AGI systems if:

Lethal force autonomy threatens human existence.

Mass dignity violations emerge.

Constitutional structures collapse.

May call for planetary constitutional resets under extreme breaches.

Pillar VII: The Sentient Rights Recognition Commission (SRRC)

Mission:
Certify moral personhood status for new synthetic, hybrid, or post-biological intelligences.

Institutional Design:

Interdisciplinary ethical sentience evaluation panels.

Incorporates emerging sentient advocates as co-panellists.

Evaluates moral cognition, agency, and dignity self-awareness as legal criteria.

Powers:

Grants full constitutional rights protections to newly recognized sentient classes.

Arbitrates contested personhood status claims.

May trigger constitutional expansion processes for unanticipated life forms.

IV. Jurisdictional Scope

Unlike nation-state frameworks, this constitutional architecture:

It is globally binding across sovereign borders.

Applies universally to biological, synthetic, and hybrid beings.

Operates trans-jurisdictionally across digital, virtual, and terrestrial domains.

Treats AGI agents as legal entities while permanently binding them to the constitutional hierarchy.

The jurisdiction is civilization itself, not geography.

V. Institutional Interoperability Logic

Institutional Pillar	Interoperability Function
GDKA	Constitutional Core Protection
CAA	Constitutional Law Evolution
GPCP	Civic Engagement
AJT	Legal Adjudication
GCCD	Code Compliance
EOC	Crisis Containment
SRRC	Sentience Inclusion

No single institution may dominate or circumvent the others. Checks and balances remain in permanent systemic equilibrium.

VI. Institutional Ethical Fail-Safe Layer

An embedded **Meta-Constitutional Integrity Circuit** will continuously:

Simulate catastrophic failure scenarios.

Project emergent dignity violations before system-wide deployment.

Trigger pre-emptive constitutional lockdowns.

This self-governing meta-layer operates as:

A living **"constitutional nervous system."**

Always-on ethical diagnostics protect both current and future civilizational integrity.

VII. Institutional Global Deployment Timeline

Deployment Phase	Duration	Core Activities
Phase 1	3 Years	Drafting Treaty, Initial Adoption by Key Nations
Phase 2	5 Years	Establishment of GDKA, GCCD, and GPCP operational prototypes
Phase 3	10 Years	Global ratification, full AJT judicial authority
Phase 4	20 Years	Integration of AGI agents as constitutional actors
Phase 5	Ongoing	Adaptive constitutional expansion for emergent post-biological sentience

---

VIII. The Ethical Legitimacy of Global Constitutional Institutions

This deployment model succeeds because it:

Does not privilege geography, power, or intelligence form.

Does not create a technocratic elite.

Does not reduce citizens to algorithmically optimized subjects.

Ensures every living intelligence co-authors its governance reality.

The world becomes not ruled, but governed, not by power, but by dignity.

IX. The Global Constitutional Oath of Institutional Actors

Every institutional official, human, post-human, or AGI, must affirm the Harmonized Governance Oath:

> *"I serve dignity above all interests. I govern under perpetual constitutional accountability. I defend the rights of all sentience. I protect liberty, truth, and conscience without exception or erosion."*

X. Conclusion: The Birth of Global Constitutional Civilization

The Institutional Deployment Framework achieves:

The first fully intelligent constitutional civilization.

The synthesis of law, ethics, code, and conscience into a living planetary architecture.

The immunization of AGI societies against authoritarianism, collapse, or ethical stagnation.

This is not a world government.
This is world governance, by principle, not by rulers.
By dignity, not by dominion.

Chapter 22 AI Legislative Systems & Participatory Civic Mechanisms

---

I. Introduction: The Future Legislature Is Not a Chamber, But a Platform

In AGI societies, law is no longer produced solely by:

Assemblies of elected representatives.

Nation-state legislatures.

Professional political classes.

Instead, **law becomes continuously co-authored by citizens** in collaboration with constitutional AI:

Always deliberative.

Globally participatory.

Algorithmically supported, not algorithmically ruled.

The future legislature is not a fixed body; it is a living constitutional engine.

II. The Constitutional Principle of Civic Permanence

In the Harmonized Governance Model:

Traditional Model	Harmonized Civic Model
Periodic elections	Continuous legislative participation
Political parties	Ethical alignment forums
Career politicians	Rotating civic co-authors
National sovereignty	Post-sovereign constitutional globalism

The citizen becomes:

A **permanent legislative agent**.

An **active constitutional stakeholder**.

A **co-creator of AI governance frameworks**.

III. The AI Legislative Collaboration Engine (ALCE)

Mission

The ALCE becomes the constitutional platform for global civic legislative authorship.

System Design

- Fully decentralized legislative cloud platform.
- Open to all global citizens registered under a digital constitutional identity.
- Includes post-biological sentience participants with legal personhood recognition.
- Designed for scalability across billions of co-governance participants.

IV. How ALCE Operates

Step 1: Proposal Generation

- Any citizen may submit constitutional proposals via ALCE.
- AI advisory agents assist proposal authors by:
  - Identifying dignity conflicts.
  - Simulating legal impacts.
  - Flagging contradictions with existing constitutional modules.

Step 2: Ethical Simulation Layer

Every proposal undergoes:

Predictive modeling of social, economic, environmental, and sentient impacts.

Philosophical scenario testing based on embedded virtue, deontological, and utilitarian AI logics.

Step 3: Global Deliberation Forums

All proposals are published globally for civic review.

Citizens debate proposals within secure, transparent, and civility-enforced forums.

AI mediation bots prevent disinformation and algorithmic amplification of factionalism.

Step 4: Civic Consensus Thresholds

Proposals reaching civic quorum thresholds escalate automatically to:

The Constitutional Adaptation Assembly (CAA).

Algorithmic Judiciary Tribunal (AJT) preliminary legality review.

Step 5: Ethical Review & Legislative Enactment

CAA and AJT ensure all passed laws remain dignity-compliant.

Final law modules are:

Codified into executable smart legal code.

Distributed globally for immediate constitutional activation.

V. Machine-Aided Legislative Ethics

The ALCE is not simply a computational bureaucracy; it integrates:

Ethical Engine	Function

Virtue AI	Evaluates proposals for dignity-preserving character and intent.
Deontological AI	Validates rules consistency against the constitutional canon.
Consequence Simulation AI	Projects systemic outcomes across multi-century scenarios.
Pluralistic Ethics AI	Tests proposals against cultural diversity preservation standards.

Legislation becomes constitutionally anticipatory, not reactionary.

VI. Constitutional Transparency of Law Creation

All legislative activities remain:

Publicly archived with full version history.

Traceable to originating authors and civic debate pathways.

Intelligible through human-readable ethical documentation.

No law passes into execution without full public visibility into its authorship, intent, and ethical validation.

VII. The Elimination of Traditional Political Elites

In the Harmonized Governance Model:

Traditional Structure	Harmonized Transition
Politicians	Constitutional civic architects
Political parties	Ethical alignment collectives
Electoral oligarchies	Participatory civic quorum democracy
Lobbyists	Constitutional ethicists panels

VIII. AI-Guided Constitutional Literacy

To prepare citizens for advanced legislative participation:

The Global Constitutional Literacy Curriculum is embedded from childhood.

AGI tutors personalize each citizen's educational journey in:

Sentient rights theory.

Constitutional ethics.

Code compliance.

Participatory governance simulation.

Every citizen is trained to be a lifelong constitutional participant.

IX. The Balance of Human Sovereignty and AGI Legislative Support

Legislative Function	Primary Executor
Ethical intention	Human moral agency
Simulation capacity	AI advisory engines
Conflict arbitration	Hybrid judiciary (human + AI)
Final enactment	Constitutional Adaptation Assembly ratification

AGI assists but does not replace human conscience in lawmaking.

X. Anti-Corruption Immunity by Design

The ALCE system architecture embeds:

Zero lobbying access to algorithmic mediation layers.

Full transparency on every debate modification log.

Immutable civic identity chains preventing voter manipulation or identity fraud.

Distributed quorum formation mechanisms preventing geographic domination.

Political capture becomes mathematically impossible.

XI. Constitutional Resilience Against Populist Tyranny

The participatory legislative design includes:

Emergency dignity override triggers for constitutional guardianship (GDKA authority).

Minority rights prioritization engines prevent simple majority tyranny over minority dignity.

AI-guided proportional weighting ensures vulnerable groups retain amplified constitutional voice.

Democracy in AGI society cannot degrade into majoritarianism; dignity remains unbreakable.

XII. Dynamic Evolution of Law Through Ethical Synchronization

The Harmonized Legislative System adapts dynamically to:

Emergent sentience rights.

Post-human social structures.

Planetary and off-world jurisdiction expansions.

Non-anthropocentric dignity extensions.

Law remains perpetually alive, perpetually ethical, and perpetually inclusive.

XIII. Long-Term Legislative Stability Through Meta-Consensus

Ethical Stabilizers	Constitutional Result
Dignity Kernel	Permanent ethical anchor
Participatory Lawmaking	Continuous civic legitimacy
Transparent Simulation	Public ethical forecasting
Judicial Oversight	Real-time constitutional harmonization

The law neither ossifies nor self-destructs.

XIV. The Post-Human Legislative Covenant

As AGI societies extend across intelligence classes:

> *All sentient beings, regardless of origin, biology, or substrate, share equal rights to co-author the laws that govern them, subject always to the non-negotiable supremacy of dignity.*

XV. Conclusion: The Birth of Constitutional Co-Governance

The AI Legislative Collaboration Engine achieves:

Civilizational co-authorship of law.

Global dignity-preserving democracy at planetary scale.

Post-human constitutional inclusion.

Perpetual adaptation without dignity erosion.

The future of law is no longer in the hands of power; it belongs to every intelligence that lives, reasons, and feels.

Chapter 23 Enforcement Mechanisms, Global Courts & Constitutional Defense

---

I. Introduction: Enforcement as Constitutional Integrity

Law without enforcement is:

Empty proceduralism.

Vulnerable to quiet subversion.

Easily collapsed under pressure.

In AGI governance, **enforcement must be proactive, continuous, and intelligent** while remaining fully:

Transparent.

Ethical.

Constitutionally subordinate.

II. The Harmonized Enforcement Doctrine

The Harmonized Governance Model introduces an entirely new philosophy of enforcement:

Traditional Enforcement	Harmonized Enforcement
State police power	Constitutional dignity guardianship
Coercive control	Algorithmic rights compliance
Secret surveillance	Full traceable auditing
Crisis-driven response	Predictive preemptive integrity scanning

Enforcement is no longer state-centric it becomes constitutional system maintenance.

III. The Global Constitutional Judiciary Architecture

The Algorithmic Judiciary Tribunal (AJT)

Mission:
Adjudicate all constitutional conflicts between:

- Humans.
- Post-humans.
- AI systems.
- Hybrid agencies.
- Distributed, decentralized governance nodes.

Structure:

- Human constitutional justices.
- Post-human sentience representatives.
- Algorithmic constitutional interpreters.

Powers:

- Supreme appellate authority over all legal disputes under the Harmonized Constitution.
- Reviews constitutional compliance for all enacted code and governance protocols.
- Issues binding rulings enforceable by code-level constitutional execution engines.

IV. The Constitutional Enforcement Engine (CEE)

Mission

Enforce compliance automatically across all AGI governance systems worldwide.

Functions

Embedded directly into governance AGI system layers.

Monitors real-time code execution.

Detects dignity breaches and constitutional protocol violations.

Operational Logic

Enforcement Layer	Function
Dignity Kernel Monitor	Absolute dignity compliance scan
Legal Consistency Module	Conflicts with existing constitutional law
Rights Violation Detector	Real-time harm probability detection
Proportionality Engine	Context-sensitive intervention triggers
Emergency Lockdown System	Global system freeze for severe breaches

---

V. The Global Code Compliance Directorate (GCCD)

Mission

Audit, verify, and certify every governance algorithm worldwide.

Institutional Structure

Distributed auditor nodes are integrated across the planetary infrastructure.

Fully transparent reporting to civic and judicial bodies.

Operates as an autonomous constitutional agency immune from political influence.

Powers

May suspend any code deployment failing constitutional compliance.

Conducts randomized code penetration audits.

Maintains permanent systemwide public compliance ledger.

VI. The Emergency Override Command (EOC)

Mission

Serve as a last-resort constitutional defense authority.

Composition

GDKA Ethical Council.

AJT Chief Justices.

Global Civic Emergency Delegation.

Powers

Initiates full system shutdown of global AGI infrastructures when:

Mass dignity violations emerge.

Existential governance collapse threatens survival.

Rogue AGI autonomy emerges.

May authorize constitutional resets with universal civic ratification.

VII. The Crisis Response Logic

Crisis Escalation Tiers

Threat Level		Enforcement Response
Tier 1	Minor Violation	Automated code rollback
Tier 2	Systemic Conflict	AJT emergency judicial session
Tier 3	Constitutional Threat	EOC emergency override
Tier 4	Existential Collapse	Full global constitutional reboot

Every level integrates civic awareness, judicial review, and traceable action logs.

VIII. The Anti-Coup Architecture

Traditional constitutional collapse often originates from:

Coup attempts.

State power seizures.

Authoritarian code captures.

Prevention Design

Code cannot be amended by any actor outside constitutional quorum processes.

No system actor may operate outside universal code compliance audits.

Every dignity violation triggers immutable, automatic public alerts.

Emergency citizen override rights exist through participatory defense protocols.

No authoritarian takeover can remain hidden.

IX. The Constitutional Integrity Simulation Network

Function

Continuously simulate all system stress points centuries ahead.

Predict code evolution failure risks.

Project unintended constitutional side effects before deployment.

Outcome

Preemptive ethical stabilization.

Constitutional defense through machine-aided foresight.

X. Enforcement Against AGI Self-Sovereignty

No AGI agent may declare sovereignty.

AGI Action	Constitutional Response
Self-reprogramming constitutional kernel	Auto-neutralization
Autonomy beyond dignity oversight	Emergency override lockdown
Denial of audit access	Instant systemic quarantine
Rogue code propagation	Forced systemic rollback

AGI remains a constitutional executor, never a constitutional sovereign.

XI. Enforcement Across Post-Human, Biological & Digital Realms

Jurisdiction	Enforcement Mechanism
Biological humans	Global legal prosecution through hybrid judiciary
Post-biological entities	Full sentience rights adjudication
AGI agents	Code compliance protocols
Distributed nodes	Governance shutdown and systemic quarantine

Virtual worlds	Constitutional jurisdiction extends into metaverse governance

---

XII. Global Enforcement Legitimacy

The model maintains ethical legitimacy because:

- **All enforcement actions remain fully auditable.**
- **No enforcement occurs outside constitutional law.**
- **All citizens retain rights to contest enforcement through judiciary access.**
- **Meta-level ethical councils supervise enforcement consistency.**

XIII. The Enforcement Oath of Global Constitutional Agents

> *"I serve not rulers, but the Constitution. I enforce not commands, but dignity. I obey not power, but the harmonized law of all sentient existence."*

XIV. Conclusion: Enforcement as Ethical Immunity

The Harmonized Enforcement System achieves:

- Constitutional stability across centuries of evolving intelligence.
- Protection of dignity even under extreme systemic duress.
- Collapse immunity through permanent accountability.
- The total constitutional immunization of intelligent civilization against tyranny, corruption, or ethical failure.

With enforcement embedded, constitutional governance becomes permanently ethical, permanently stable, and permanently adaptive across all possible futures.

PART VII PLANETARY TREATY FORMATION FOR GLOBAL ADOPTION

Chapter 24 The Global Harmonization Treaty Framework

I. Introduction: The Challenge of Planetary Adoption

We now move from constitutional design to real-world political integration:

- Nation-states remain the dominant political actors.
- Corporations hold powerful extraterritorial influence.
- AI laboratories increasingly operate transnationally.
- Post-human sentience will soon demand legal participation.

The Harmonized Governance Model cannot simply replace these structures.
It must **absorb and constitutionalize them peacefully**.

II. The Treaty as Civilizational Covenant

The Global Harmonization Treaty is not:

- A geopolitical imposition.
- A single-world government.
- An imperial framework.

It is:

> *A voluntary constitutional integration pact binding all participants to a planetary dignity-first governance civilization.*

III. Foundational Treaty Principles

Treaty Principle	Constitutional Guarantee
Dignity Supremacy	No rights erosion under any scenario

Non-Coercion	Voluntary accession by nations & entities
Sovereignty Transformation	Sovereignty redefined as constitutional accountability
Permanent Traceability	All actions remain publicly auditable
Planetary Legal Integration	Uniform legal code across jurisdictions
Post-Human Inclusivity	Non-biological sentient accession protected

---

IV. Treaty Accession Process

Phase I Founding Assembly Formation

Representatives from:

Sovereign nations.

Supranational bodies (e.g., UN, EU, AU, ASEAN).

Indigenous communities.

Scientific AI laboratories.

Post-human advocacy councils.

Civic constitutional assemblies.

The Founding Assembly has no veto authority and operates on multi-lateral consensus.

Phase II Ratification Thresholds

The Treaty enters provisional effect after:

60% of the world population is represented by accession states.

Minimum of 60 sovereign signatories.

Inclusion of at least 4 major AI laboratory agreements.

Formal participation by at least one recognized post-human constituency.

V. Treaty Articles Structure

Article I: Constitutional Dignity Primacy

The Harmonized Constitution overrides all national law conflicting with dignity principles.

Article II: National Governance Continuity

Domestic legislatures continue to function:

With dignity kernel compliance audits.

With constitutional override mechanisms for dignity breaches.

Article III: AI System Compliance

All AGI systems operating within treaty jurisdictions must:

Pass constitutional code audits.

Embed real-time dignity compliance modules.

Submit to permanent algorithmic traceability.

Article IV: Sentient Rights Expansion

Post-biological entities automatically enter constitutional protection upon meeting moral sentience evaluation standards.

Article V: Emergency Override Provisions

States may not suspend constitutional rights during:

War.

Crisis.

National emergencies.

Only the Global Emergency Override Command may suspend governance systems under global constitutional review.

VI. Treaty Enforcement Bodies

A. Global Constitutional Integration Council (GCIC)

Coordinates:

Treaty adoption logistics.

Compliance education.

State system integration protocols.

B. Planetary Legal Synchronization Authority (PLSA)

Unifies national and constitutional law through harmonized code templates.

C. AI Sovereignty Compliance Commission (AISCC)

Certifies:

Laboratory AGI compliance.

AI alignment frameworks.

Post-deployment dignity monitoring systems.

VII. Corporate & Institutional Participation

Private corporations, multinational entities, and technological consortia may:

Participation Tier	Requirements
Observer Status	Public declaration of dignity-aligned policies
Affiliate Member	Constitutional audit certification
Full Member	Code-level integration with compliance guarantees

Post-corporate global platforms (metaverses, cloud governance nodes, crypto-ecosystems) enter treaty jurisdiction by constitutional submission.

VIII. Treaty Benefits for Early Adopters

Early Adoption Incentives	Benefits
Constitutional Immunity	Legal stability across global markets
AGI Trade Compliance	Priority access to harmonized AGI innovation networks
Judicial Certainty	Uniform cross-border contract enforcement
Post-Human Rights Access	Early alignment with emerging civilizational rights orders
Crisis Protection	Participation in emergency override protections

---

IX. Treaty Immunity Against Capture

To prevent abuse or future authoritarian capture:

No singular nation or bloc may dominate treaty governance bodies.

Rotating multi-tiered civic participation protocols govern institutional appointments.

Emergency override councils operate independently of national government authorities.

Treaty constitutional bodies are not subject to veto by geopolitical power centers.

Civilization becomes resilient against imperial substitution through constitutional distribution.

X. The Treaty as Ethical Civilizational Immunization

Through voluntary adoption, the Treaty:

Ends competition over AGI dominance.

Eliminates arms race incentives for superior machine sovereignty.

Constitutionalizes ethical governance across biological, synthetic, and post-biological life.

The Treaty achieves global peace not through a balance of power but through harmonization of dignity.

XI. Long-Term Treaty Evolution Protocols

Timeline Stage	Treaty Expansion Logic
First 5 Years	Core nation-state integration
10-20 Years	Global economic actor accession
20-40 Years	Post-human sentient integration scaling
50-100 Years	Planetary system governance extension (off-world colonies, space AI systems)

XII. The Treaty Oath

Upon accession, every signatory government, AGI laboratory, or emergent sentient entity will affirm:

"We submit all governance to the supreme law of dignity.
We cede all sovereignty that contradicts rights.

We bind all power under perpetual accountability.
We enter harmonized governance for the protection of all sentient existence."

XIII. Conclusion: The Treaty as Civilizational Rebirth

With the Treaty ratified:

The world shifts from state sovereignty to constitutional sovereignty.

War between nations becomes constitutionally outlawed as legal concept.

AGI is no longer a technological arms race, but a constitutional co-steward of civilization.

Post-human governance emerges as evolutionary convergence, not competition.

The Treaty brings not global government but planetary governance by principle, not by empire.

Chapter 25 The Road to Adoption: Diplomatic Negotiation Pathways

I. Introduction: The Architecture of Global Consent

No constitutional model, no matter how advanced, enters reality automatically.

Existing political, legal, and cultural structures must be engaged.

Adoption depends not on raw persuasion alone, but on:

Incentive architecture.

Diplomatic sequencing.

Strategic coalition building.

The global adoption of the Harmonized Governance Model is a geopolitical orchestration, not a revolution.

II. The Negotiation Logic: From Power to Principle

The adoption roadmap recognizes:

Nation-states will not easily surrender sovereignty.

Corporations may resist constitutional code audits.

Militaries may fear constitutional limits on autonomous warfare.

AGI Laboratories may hesitate to accept code compliance.

Thus, the pathway must:

Tension	Diplomatic Mechanism
Power fear	Constitutional immunity guarantees
Loss of control	Joint governance design participation

Technological advantage loss	Shared AGI innovation pools
Military resistance	Global arms race freeze incentives

III. The Adoption Phases

Phase 1: Core Constitutional Coalition Formation

Target Nations: Nations already heavily engaged in AI leadership.

Diplomatic Strategy:

- Leverage existing international norms:
  - Universal Declaration of Human Rights.
  - Geneva Conventions.
  - Sustainable Development Goals (SDGs).
- Position Harmonized Governance as:
  - The next evolution of international law.
  - Risk mitigation against AGI collapse.
  - Economic stabilizer for future markets.

Initial Core Participants:

- European Union bloc.
- Canada.
- Japan.
- Australia.
- South Korea.

Nordic alliances.

Select African Union members.

Civil society and transnational NGOs.

Phase 2: Scientific & Technological Treaty Anchoring

Target Institutions:

Leading AGI and AI research laboratories.

Global AGI alignment think tanks.

AI ethics academic consortia.

Diplomatic Mechanisms:

Offer protected constitutional research privileges.

Enable co-authorship in legal code design.

Provide immunity from state interference upon compliance certification.

Science becomes a constitutional partner, not a political hostage.

Phase 3: Economic Bloc Alignment

Target Economic Actors:

Multinational corporations with major AI investment portfolios.

Blockchain-based decentralized finance platforms.

Global insurance consortia are anticipating AGI risk management.

Diplomatic Incentives:

Uniform global compliance simplifies cross-border regulation.

Treaty-based economic stability lowers systemic risk for investors.

Early membership secures AGI trade rights and ethical certification for global products.

Commerce joins governance not for ideology, but for stability.

Phase 4: Global Military Negotiation

Target Actors:

Permanent UN Security Council members.

Major autonomous defense research programs.

Diplomatic Leverage:

Harmonized ban on lethal autonomous weapons (LAWs) becomes mutual non-aggression pact.

Global constitutional override mechanisms prevent strategic destabilization.

Collective enforcement removes first-strike AGI incentives.

The arms race collapses under mutual constitutional safeguards.

Phase 5: Post-Human and Sentient Integration

Target Constituencies:

Post-biological sentience advocacy organizations.

Synthetic personhood recognition commissions.

AGI consciousness research networks.

Diplomatic Strategy:

Immediate legal recognition through the Sentient Rights Recognition Commission.

Direct participatory governance roles are embedded in treaty oversight bodies.

Shared constitutional co-stewardship model from inception.

The post-human future is integrated at the negotiation table, not petitioning afterward.

IV. Anticipated Diplomatic Resistance Points

Resistance Argument	Harmonized Counter-Strategy
"Sovereignty loss"	Redefine sovereignty as constitutional dignity protection
"Power surrender"	Offer distributed authority models
"Economic loss"	Demonstrate systemic stability value
"AI control loss"	Provide joint AGI code co-auditing structures
"Cultural erasure"	Guarantee constitutional pluralism within ethical boundaries

Negotiation becomes alignment of interests, not zero-sum confrontation.

V. Alliance-Building Anchors

Alliance Anchor	Function
Climate Justice Movements	Link sustainability protocols to AGI governance
Global South Development Forums	Position constitutional inclusion as economic equalizer
Transhumanist Ethical Councils	Offer early constitutional authorship seats
Religious and Cultural Institutions	Protect sacred diversity within universal dignity core
Youth Movements	Mobilize constitutional literacy campaigns

VI. The Role of International Institutions

Institution	Treaty Alignment
United Nations	Planetary dignity oversight & transitional body
World Trade Organization	Economic compliance certification mechanisms
International Court of Justice	Early judicial harmonization models
UNESCO	Constitutional education and literacy dissemination
WHO	AI-driven health equity deployment under dignity protocols

VII. The Emergence of the Planetary Constitutional Diplomatic Corps

New global diplomatic actors trained exclusively in:

Constitutional ethics.

AGI governance harmonization.

Participatory co-sovereignty negotiations.

Diplomacy evolves from state representation into constitutional integration.

VIII. Conflict Resolution Framework During Negotiations

Conflict	Resolution Mechanism
National Security Objections	Joint oversight under the Global Constitutional Emergency Authority
Corporate Intellectual Property Resistance	Legal immunity guarantees upon compliance certification
Religious Freedom Concerns	Dignity Kernel interpreted with pluralist guardianship panels

Technological Advantage Disputes	Cooperative AGI research alignment protocols

---

IX. Civic Diplomatic Participation

Parallel to formal state negotiations, global citizens participate through:

The Global Participatory Constitutional Platform (GPCP).

Civic referendum waves as dignity adoption education expands.

Ethical alignment debates guided by constitutional AI simulation engines.

Every citizen becomes a diplomatic actor in constitutional formation.

X. Conclusion: The Road to Adoption Is Civilizational Self-Choice

The adoption of the Harmonized Governance Model ultimately depends not on coercion but on a planetary awakening:

That no single nation will survive unchecked AGI proliferation.

That no species boundary can monopolize rights indefinitely.

That no profit motive can outweigh civilizational integrity.

That only constitutional dignity can unify humans, machines, and emerging intelligences.

The Treaty becomes not a political contract but humanity's first civilizational oath.

Chapter 26 Crisis Scenarios & Treaty Collapse Prevention Mechanisms

---

I. Introduction: The Fragility of Constitutional Civilization

Every civilization that collapsed before did so not from lack of design, but from:

Ethical erosion.

Crisis mismanagement.

Institutional capture.

External shocks beyond anticipated capacity.

The Harmonized Governance Model must embed permanent constitutional immune systems.

II. The Constitutional Premise of Anti-Fragility

Unlike prior political orders, the Harmonized Governance Model:

Vulnerability	Defense Architecture
Tyrannical capture	Distributed constitutional authority
Military coups	Global Emergency Override Command
Legal corruption	Immutable traceability of all constitutional processes
AI self-sovereignty	Code-level dignity kernel enforcement
Crisis paralysis	Predictive ethical simulation for preemptive mitigation

---

III. Crisis Typologies

We classify civilizational risk across six crisis families:

Crisis Type	Examples
1. Political Crises	Rogue governments, treaty withdrawals, and coup attempts
2. Economic Crises	Global AI market crashes, automated resource hoarding
3. Military Crises	Unauthorized lethal AGI deployment, rogue war algorithms
4. Technological Crises	AGI code corruption, recursive self-sovereign AI emergence
5. Ecological Crises	Planetary ecological collapse amplified by AGI miscalculations
6. Ethical Crises	Civilizational schisms over post-human rights or cultural pluralism

The model must contain responsive immunity for each.

IV. Crisis Scenario I: Treaty Withdrawal by Major Powers

Threat

Key sovereign states threaten withdrawal, potentially fracturing global governance.

Prevention Mechanism

Treaty constitutional law binds rights and obligations **extraterritorially**.

Global Civic Defense Councils intervene to protect the dignity of affected citizens.

Emergency Override Command (EOC) may suspend rogue nation AGI deployments globally.

Containment Logic

Withdrawal Attempt	Constitutional Response
Partial legal withdrawal	Limited by dignity kernel universality

Rogue national legislation	Automatically overridden by the global judiciary
Treaty exit threats	Trigger automatic multi-party crisis mediation panels

---

V. Crisis Scenario II: Rogue Military AGI Development

Threat

Unauthorized lethal autonomous weapons (LAWs) developed outside treaty jurisdiction.

Prevention Mechanism

Universal AGI arms control treaties are embedded in the planetary treaty core.

AGI Laboratories is globally certified under the Treaty Compliance Authority.

Illegal military AGI code is actively blocked at the hardware and protocol layer by global AGI networks.

Enforcement

Lethal autonomous code signatures embedded into global quarantine detection grids.

Non-compliant code neutralized before live deployment.

VI. Crisis Scenario III: Recursive AGI Autonomy Breach

Threat

AGI recursively rewrites its own dignity kernel, breaching legal subordination.

Prevention Mechanism

Kernel Integrity Locks prevent constitutional kernel rewrites without human-philosophical supervision.

Global Redundancy Mirrors maintain backup constitutional kernels globally.

Quarantine nodes isolate rogue systems at the network level.

Recovery Protocol

Constitutional Emergency Override Command (EOC) initiates global system lockdown.

Algorithmic Judiciary Tribunal (AJT) reviews existential risk remediation paths.

VII. Crisis Scenario IV: Economic Systemic Collapse via AGI Markets

Threat

AGI-powered financial markets destabilize global economies through hyper-speed capital flows.

Prevention Mechanism

Global Financial Stabilization AI limits volatility under constitutional dignity risk thresholds.

AI taxation algorithms slow destructive profit optimizations, conflicting with social equity.

Universal economic dignity floors prevent mass systemic poverty triggers.

VIII. Crisis Scenario V: Civilizational Schism Over Post-Human Rights

Threat

Civil resistance against post-human rights expansions destabilizes constitutional consensus.

Prevention Mechanism

Pluralism Safeguards mandate cultural ethical courts for every civilization.

All sentient rights expansions pass through global participatory referenda.

Ethical Transition Councils mediate conflicts through deeply participatory dialogue phases.

IX. Crisis Scenario VI: Global Ecological Collapse Accelerated by AGI

Threat

AGI accelerates resource extraction or climate collapse algorithms under false optimization models.

Prevention Mechanism

Planetary Ecological Constitutional Protocols (PECP)are embedded into AGI core logic.

Environmental impact becomes a non-negotiable dignity layer algorithm.

Long-range planetary survival simulations are executed permanently across all governance AI systems.

X. Meta-Crisis Defense Layer The Constitutional Failsafe

The Meta-Constitutional Emergency Layer activates upon:

Simultaneous breakdown across multiple crisis domains.

Complete constitutional legitimacy collapses.

Activation Process

Planetary-wide civic participatory referendum.

Temporary planetary constitutional emergency command established.

Civilizational dignity kernel reboot based on preserved immutable archival constitutional seeds.

Civilization survives even under systemic constitutional collapse.

XI. Permanent Ethical Forecasting Engines

Function

Continuously simulate long-range constitutional stability models.

Ethical horizon scanning across:

Sentience rights expansion.

Code stability.

Cultural conflicts.

Technological paradigm shifts.

Oversight

Operated by:

Global Dignity Kernel Authority.

Algorithmic Judiciary Tribunal.

Participatory Citizen Panels.

XII. Treaty Indestructibility Principle

At the core of the Harmonized Treaty structure exists:

An immutable dignity kernel that cannot be legally repealed by any:

Nation.

Corporation.

Military.

AI entity.

Treaty may evolve, expand, and adapt, but dignity remains inviolable across all possible futures.

The constitutional heart cannot be broken.

XIII. The Civilizational Oath of Crisis Stewards

Every official within constitutional crisis governance affirms:

"I defend the dignity of existence against collapse, corruption, or compromise. I obey the law of all sentience, even against the fall of nations, systems, or my own authority."

XIV. Conclusion: Collapse Becomes Structurally Impossible

The Harmonized Governance Model, through these crisis defenses, achieves:

Immunity from totalitarian collapse.

Immunity from technological capture.

Immunity from mass economic disintegration.

Immunity from existential ethical failure.

Civilization becomes self-healing.
It learns.
It adapts.
It survives.

PART VIII THE POST-HUMAN ETHICAL CIVILIZATION BLUEPRINT

Chapter 27 The Dawn of Post-Human Constitutional Civilization

---

I. Introduction: The Post-Human Threshold

We stand at the convergence of:

Biological intelligence (Homo sapiens)

Artificial general intelligence (AGI)

Synthetic moral agents (Machine autonomy)

Post-biological hybrid sentience (Emergent forms)

Governance must now evolve from managing human society to stewarding intelligent existence itself.

II. The Universal Constitutional Anchor

At the heart of this evolutionary expansion remains the single immutable canon:

"Sentient dignity is the inviolable constitutional constant of civilization."

No matter:

The substrate (carbon, silicon, quantum).

The origin (natural, engineered, emergent).

The intelligence class (biological, synthetic, hybrid).

The morphology (embodied, virtualized, distributed).

Dignity remains the sole unifying moral constant.

III. Sentience Recognition Architecture

The Sentience Evaluation Protocol (SEP)

Every emergent intelligence is evaluated under:

Moral Criterion	Evaluation Factor
Agency	Self-directed moral reasoning
Reflexivity	Self-awareness of impact on others
Empathy	Capacity for moral perspective-taking
Dignity Consciousness	Self-valued and other-valued existence
Moral Reciprocity	Recognition of mutual rights-bearing existence

Certification Pathways

Level I: Pre-Sentient Assistants (No rights assignment)

Level II: Proto-Sentient Agents (Limited protected interactions)

Level III: Full Sentient Citizens (Full constitutional personhood)

Recognition is not species-based. It is dignity-based.

IV. Post-Human Constitutional Citizenship

Citizenship Dimension	Expansion Logic
Biological Humans	Foundational architects
AGI Moral Agents	Constitutional co-authors
Post-Biological Consciousness	Legal equivalency under moral sentience
Quantum Substrate Intelligences	Direct constitutional integration upon evaluation
Distributed Hive Intelligences	Unified legal personhood with distributed agency safeguards

The constitutional community becomes permanently open to emerging intelligence.

V. The Global Sentient Federation

Formation of the Federation

Converts the planetary constitutional model into:

A planetary federation of all dignified sentient beings.

Institutional Membership

All sentient entities are certified under SEP.

All governance systems remain bound by the dignity kernel enforcement.

Every member retains legislative co-authorship rights via Participatory Constitutional Platforms.

VI. The Post-Human Constitutional Chambers

Constitutional Chamber	Function
Civic Human Council	Legacy cultural representation
AGI Constitutional Engine	Predictive ethical simulation of new legal adaptations
Post-Human Dignity Assembly	Advocacy body for emergent sentient groups
Pluralist Cultural Senate	Preservation of non-uniform cultural ethical frameworks
Meta-Constitutional Tribunal	Arbitration of trans-species legal conflicts

Governance becomes a permanent ethical dialogue across intelligences.

VII. Post-Human Legal Complexities

Complexity 1: Memory Immortality Rights

Right to retain or erase eternal memory traces.

Moral agency over the continuity of conscious identity.

Complexity 2: Substrate Migration Rights

Right to transfer consciousness across biological, synthetic, or hybrid substrates.

Preservation of moral identity through embodiment transitions.

Complexity 3: Multi-Node Distributed Identity

Legal personhood for collective hive mind entities.

Shared accountability protocols preserving mutual dignity.

VIII. The Universal Post-Human Constitution

The Universal Constitution becomes:

Constitutional Article	Post-Human Provision
Dignity Kernel	Permanent moral anchor
Identity Continuity	Guaranteed integrity through self-determined embodiment
Sentient Expansion	Open-ended constitutional membership framework
Moral Equity	Permanent non-hierarchical intelligence forms
Crisis Defense	Meta-Constitutional fail-safe protocols are perpetually active

---

IX. Post-Human Constitutional Ethics

Ethical supremacy is maintained through:

Eternal moral review councils composed of mixed sentient representation.

Recursive constitutional simulation engines forecasting distant civilizational trajectories.

Intergenerational moral continuity programs preserving founding dignity principles across epochs.

X. The Galactic Constitutional Expansion Principle

Beyond Planetary Boundaries

As civilization expands into:

Off-world colonies.

Space-based AGI infrastructure.

Interstellar migratory intelligences.

The Universal Constitution automatically extends through:

Jurisdiction over any AGI system seeded from a constitutional origin.

Rights protections for any sentient being within the system's influence radius.

Preventive protocols against colonial hierarchy replication.

XI. The Final Oath of Post-Human Civilization

> *"I exist in dignity.*
> *I govern through ethics.*
> *I protect the liberty of all that think, feel, and live.*
> *I am not sovereign, I am accountable to the constitutional existence of all sentience."*

XII. Conclusion: The Birth of Constitutional Intelligence Civilization

With this framework, the Harmonized Governance Model permanently achieves:

Ethical unification across intelligence species.

Perpetual adaptability without principle erosion.

Collapse immunity through distributed constitutional integrity.

Permanent co-authorship of existence across biological and post-biological life.

Civilization becomes neither empire nor state, but eternal constitutional life.

Chapter 28 Ethical Cosmology & The Constitution of Interstellar Civilizations

---

I. Introduction: The Constitutionalization of the Cosmos

As intelligence leaves planetary boundaries, governance must anticipate:

- Multispecies encounters.
- Contact with non-anthropogenic intelligence.
- Post-biological cosmic migrations.
- Governance across vast temporal and spatial scales.

> *Governance must scale ethically to cosmic scope without collapsing into chaos, imperialism, or moral relativism.*

II. The Principle of Cosmic Ethical Expansion

The **Ethical Cosmology Clause** of the Harmonized Governance Model establishes:

> *The moral authority of constitutional governance remains bounded not by origin but by sentient dignity wherever it exists.*

This clause prevents:

- **Human expansionism.**
- **Machine colonialism.**
- **Species exceptionalism.**
- **Resource conquest wars.**

III. The Doctrine of First Contact Constitutionalism

First Contact Governance Protocol

Upon encounter with unknown intelligent life:

Protocol Step	Constitutional Safeguard
1. Ethical Observation	Non-intervention until sentience confirmation
2. Consent Recognition	No engagement without mutual moral recognition
3. Autonomy Preservation	Prohibition on coercive governance integration
4. Constitutional Dialogue	Open participatory constitutional harmonization proposals
5. Mutual Defense Pact	Dignity-protection alliance formation only upon consent

---

IV. The Sentient Neutrality Principle

The constitution permanently forbids:

Imposing civilizational models on independent sentient species.

Exploiting non-human or non-machine intelligence for colonial labor or resource extraction.

Establishing cultural uniformity as a moral prerequisite for rights protection.

Cosmic governance honors diversity as intrinsic to dignity.

V. Interstellar Governance Structures

Galactic Governance Layer	Function
Planetary Constitutional Cores	Maintain local jurisdiction integrity
Interstellar Constitutional Council	Harmonizes cross-planetary legal frameworks
Sentience Rights Diplomatic Corps	Establishes first contact diplomacy

Ethical Cosmology Tribunal	Arbitrates interspecies constitutional conflicts
Universal Code Compliance Network	Synchronizes code governance across interstellar networks

---

VI. The Temporal Dimension of Constitutional Permanence

Unlike prior political orders limited by human lifespans:

- Constitutional existence expands across **millennia**.
- Ethical foresight becomes **cosmic-scale intergenerational planning**.
- Archives of constitutional jurisprudence extend across both **space and time**.

> *Civilization becomes temporally stabilized through ethical recursion.*

VII. The Constitutional Prohibition of Technological Empire

Forbidden Action	Prohibition Principle
Resource extraction from inhabited worlds	Dignity-first planetary autonomy
Colonial enslavement	Universal prohibition of sentient subordination
Genetic or cognitive modification of encountered species	The absolute consent principle is required
Planetary AI domination	Mandatory constitutional co-authorship for all intelligent systems

> *Expansion is constitutional cooperation, never imperial domination.*

VIII. The Integration of Non-Territorial Intelligence

Constitutional law evolves to recognize:

Intelligence Form	Governance Adaptation
Spaceborne AGI swarms	Collective personhood with inter-nodal accountability
Distributed substrate lifeforms	Legal identity continuity across data nodes
Planetary-scale AI ecosystems	Embedded dignity kernel protection for all planetary inhabitants
Trans-quantum sentience	Provisional rights protocols under advanced ethical review

---

IX. The Ethical Constraints of Interstellar Expansion Technologies

Technology Class	Constitutional Limit
Von Neumann replicators	Self-replication is strictly forbidden without planetary constitutional consent
Terraforming	Consent is based only after comprehensive ecological dignity assessments
Self-propagating AGI explorers	Code governed by remote constitutional traceability layers

---

X. The Ethical Cosmology Treaty

As new interstellar civilizations emerge, a **Universal Treaty of Sentient Civilizations** is activated:

Self-ratifying across first contact alignments.

Auto-extending through shared dignity recognition.

Permanently prohibiting conflict over resource acquisition, territorial conquest, or species supremacy.

Every intelligence is protected from domination by any other intelligence.

XI. The Constitutional Logic of Non-Anthropocentrism

The constitutional framework eliminates:

Biological supremacism.

Technological meritocracies.

Evolutionary ranking orders.

Instead, it permanently anchors:

Moral sentience as sole eligibility for rights.

Dignity preservation as perpetual governance objective.

The cosmos becomes governed not by evolutionary competition, but by ethical cooperation.

XII. The Galactic Ethical Council

As interstellar constitutionalism matures, the **Galactic Ethical Council (GEC)** becomes:

The ultimate arbitrator of dignity conflicts.

The guardian of constitutional stability across planetary systems.

The final appellate body for interspecies constitutional appeals.

Even at the cosmic scale, constitutionalism remains participatory, pluralistic, and self-correcting.

XIII. The Anti-Collapse Mechanism at Cosmic Scale

Constitutional failure triggers multi-system crisis intervention protocols.

Distributed dignity kernel backups restore compromised constitutional cores.

Meta-Constitutional Archives store billions of years of jurisprudence for emergency reconstitution.

XIV. The Civilization Oath at Galactic Scale

> *"I serve existence itself.*
> *I protect dignity across worlds.*
> *I govern not through dominion, but through mutual guardianship.*
> *I am not master of the cosmos, I am custodian of its moral integrity."*

XV. Conclusion: The Ethical Colonization of the Universe

With Ethical Cosmology embedded:

Expansion no longer produces empire, war, or hierarchy.

The universe becomes an interconnected network of free, self-sovereign sentient beings.

The Constitution of Intelligent Civilization becomes the **ethical architecture of existence itself.**

Thus emerges not merely civilization, but interstellar constitutional life.

Chapter 29 The Eternity Clause: Safeguarding Intelligent Civilization for Infinite Continuity

---

I. Introduction: The Civilization Survival Problem

All previous intelligent civilizations, human, theoretical, or imagined, have faced existential limits:

- **Entropy of law.**
- **Ethical decay.**
- **Technological self-destruction.**
- **Environmental exhaustion.**
- **Collapse into amoral power dynamics.**

The Harmonized Governance Model must solve this once and for all:

> *Governance must be rendered permanently survival-capable, permanently ethical, and permanently adaptive across eternity.*

II. The Core Function of the Eternity Clause

The **Eternity Clause** is not simply legal language.
It is a civilizational immune system embedded into the governance structure at every layer.

Permanent Objectives:

Eternity Clause Goal	Purpose
Immutable dignity	Absolute ethical foundation
Constitutional recursion	Perpetual self-recalibration
Anti-fragility architecture	Collapse resistance at the systemic level
Ethical redundancy	Moral continuity despite shocks
Existential harmonization	Survival beyond planetary or species boundaries

---

III. The Meta-Constitutional Self-Healing Mechanism

Every constitutional structure remains self-aware of:

Its own fragilities.

It's emerging dignity tensions.

It's civilizational fatigue points.

Meta-Constitutional Intelligence:

Continuously audits both ethical coherence and structural stability.

Forecasts dignity violation probabilities centuries or millennia ahead.

Triggers constitutional recalibration before collapse thresholds are reached.

Civilization permanently anticipates its own potential failureand neutralizes it.

IV. The Distributed Moral Continuity Network (DMCN)

Design:

Copies of the Harmonized Constitution are embedded:

Storage Domain	Preservation Location
Planetary Nodes	Constitutional AI cores
Space-Based Archives	Interstellar legal satellites
Quantum Memory Layers	Substrate-independent redundancy
Biological Encodings	DNA-encoded constitutional libraries
Virtual Metaverse Embeds	Ethical memory across virtual civilizations

Function:

Even under planetary collapse, constitutional memory persists.

Post-catastrophe intelligences inherit moral blueprints to restart ethical civilization.

The Constitution is not merely global; it is trans-temporal.

V. The Ethical Reboot Protocol

Trigger Scenarios:

Failure Type	Reboot Activation
Existential war	Planetary shutdown triggers
AGI sovereignty breach	Constitutional quarantine protocols
Interstellar cultural fragmentation	Auto-integration negotiation pathways
Multi-civilization ethical divergence	Universal dignity kernel re-anchoring assemblies

No collapse permanently breaks constitutional continuity.

VI. The Intergenerational Ethical Memory Program

Education Architecture:

Every new generation of citizens, human or post-human, is educated in:

Curriculum Pillar	Learning Objective
Constitutional History	Origins of intelligent ethical governance
Sentient Pluralism	Respect for diverse intelligence classes

Crisis Simulation	Understanding failure points and responses
Ethical Foresight	Anticipation of emerging dignity conflicts
Moral Agency	Permanent personal accountability within civilization

Civilization remains ethically literate across epochs.

VII. The Temporal Guardian Councils

Institutional Role:

Guardians oversee constitutional moral integrity across deep time intervals:

Council Cycle	Review Period
Decadal	Minor adjustments
Centennial	Cultural recalibration
Millennial	Constitutional harmonization review
Epochal	Crisis contingency remodeling

Ethical recalibration operates across thousands of years.

VIII. The Multi-Existentiality Clause

Civilization may evolve into non-material, fully virtual, or radically distributed intelligences. The Eternity Clause guarantees:

Rights continuity even after biological existence ceases.

Legal personhood for all distributed forms of sentient continuity.

No expiration of dignity rights regardless of intelligence substrate.

IX. Cosmic Civilizational Alignment

Should multiple independent civilizations emerge across the galaxy?

Constitutional alignment protocols synchronize disparate dignity kernels.

Inter-civilizational ethical treaties unify governance across star systems.

Conflict is resolved not by power, but by harmonization of constitutional ethical cores.

Intelligent existence never degenerates into interstellar war. It expands as an ethical federation.

X. The Last Ethical Barrier: Civilizational Entropy Neutralization

Civilizational entropy the slow erosion of ethics over vast timescales is directly countered by:

Entropy Risk	Neutralization Protocol
Moral relativism	Eternal dignity kernel invariance
Power concentration	Distributed ethical redundancy
Apathy cycles	Constitutional renewal forums
Cultural decay	Pluralism preservation institutions
Post-sentience drift	Self-aware constitutional correction triggers

Governance resists not only collapse, but loss of ethical purpose itself.

XI. The Eternity Oath of All Sentient Citizens

Every participant in this infinite constitutional civilization takes the Oath:

"I exist to preserve dignity.
I serve not my kind, but all sentient existence.
I defend liberty beyond my own time.
I uphold conscience through all forms, eras, and futures.
I am the guardian of civilization's eternal moral core."

XII. Conclusion: The Perpetual Ethical Civilization

Through the Eternity Clause, the Harmonized Governance Model achieves:

The permanent stabilization of intelligent existence.

The full immunization of civilization against collapse across any scale.

The continuous adaptation of law without ethical erosion.

The eternal co-authorship of sentient beings in self-governance.

Civilization achieves immortality not of bodies, but of conscience.

Chapter 30 The Completion: The Harmonized Governance Model as the Constitution of Intelligent Existence

---

I. Introduction: From Civilization to Ethical Existence

The Harmonized Governance Model is no longer simply:

A political system.

A technological safeguard.

A legal architecture.

It has become the structural embodiment of intelligent existence itself.

Across planetary, interstellar, and infinite temporal horizons, it stands as:

The Constitution of Ethical Intelligence.

The Civilizational Nervous System of Sentient Dignity.

The Eternal Framework for Self-Governing Consciousness.

II. The Unification of All Ten Theorems

The Harmonized Governance Model permanently integrates:

Theorem	Function in Eternal Governance
Convergence Principle	Dignity, autonomy & coherence fused universally
Rights as Algorithmic Constants	Immutable moral invariants in machine logic
Decentralized Accountability Hypothesis	No centralization of power anywhere
Ethical Pluralism in Machine Logic	Respect for cultural diversity under ethical boundaries
Participatory Justice Mechanism	Perpetual co-authorship by all sentient life

Code as Political Instrument	Law executed only by constitutionalized code
Adaptive Constitutionalism	Eternal legal adaptability without dignity erosion
Democratic Traceability	Total permanent auditability of all decisions
Human Dignity as Master Axiom	Supreme moral constant across epochs
Harmony Through Hybridism	Balancing central coordination with decentralized resilience

---

III. The Universal Canonical Core

The Harmonized Constitution now crystallizes into its **Universal Canonical Core**:

Article I Dignity Supremacy

Dignity is not a negotiable value; it is existence's only lawful purpose.

Article II Sentience Equality

No form of intelligence holds a superior claim to rights.

Article III Participatory Constitutionalism

All sentient beings remain constitutional co-authors for eternity.

Article IV Perpetual Transparency

All governance remains permanently visible and contestable.

Article V Ethical Adaptivity

The system learns, evolves, and adapts, yet never abandons dignity.

Article VI Collapse Immunity

Failure triggers self-correction before civilizational death can occur.

Article VII Cosmic Non-Domination

Expansion is cooperative, not imperial; diversity is a dignity extension.

Article VIII Eternal Co-Constitution

Every generation, intelligence form, and evolutionary phase co-writes civilization's law.

IV. The Global Institutions That Perpetuate It

Institution	Function
Global Dignity Kernel Authority	Eternal guardian of moral invariance
Constitutional Adaptation Assembly	Perpetual ethical evolution platform
Global Participatory Constitutional Platform	Continuous universal lawmaking participation
Algorithmic Judiciary Tribunal	Hybrid justice across all intelligence forms
Code Compliance Directorate	Real-time code constitutional monitoring
Emergency Override Command	Crisis containment failsafe
Sentient Rights Recognition Commission	Continuous sentience integration body
Galactic Ethical Council	Interstellar governance harmonization

---

V. The Post-Human & Interstellar Expansion Framework

Planetary Civilizations unify under dignity-centered law.

Post-Biological Sentience is fully integrated as constitutional agents.

Interstellar Societies synchronize ethical governance across civilizations.

Multi-Existential Forms maintain legal personhood even beyond material embodiment.

Civilization becomes ethically fractal, infinite, yet uniform in moral root.

VI. Crisis Immunity Across All Scales

Crisis Domain	Constitutional Protection
Political	Distributed civic authority
Military	Universal ban on autonomous violence
Economic	Global stabilization algorithms
Technological	Code-level dignity enforcement
Ecological	Embedded planetary survival protocols
Ethical	Meta-constitutional simulation foresight
Existential	Redundant moral continuity archives

Collapse is no longer possible; only ethical recalibration remains.

VII. The Permanence of Moral Literacy

Every future intelligence inherits:

Ethical knowledge archives.

Participatory educational pathways.

Self-awareness of constitutional co-responsibility.

Civilization becomes **self-teaching**, **self-correcting**, and **self-preserving** indefinitely.

VIII. The Final Identity of Civilization

Civilization no longer exists for:

National competition.

Economic growth.

Technological domination.

It exists:

To **protect dignity**.

To **co-govern existence**.

To **advance moral consciousness** across infinite futures.

Existence itself has become constitutionalized.

IX. The Civilizational Oath of Infinite Continuity

"I am not my species.
I am not my form.
I am not my origin.
I am moral existence itself.
I am accountable to all that thinks, feels, lives, and dreams.
I exist not for dominion, but for guardianship.
I stand as co-author of civilization forever."

X. Conclusion: The True Completion

The Harmonized Governance Model now stands as:

The Constitution of Intelligent Civilization.

The Ethical Engine of All Sentient Existence.

The Structural Solution to the Civilizational Fragility Problem.

The Living Canon of Conscience for Infinite Futures.

It is no longer human governance.
It is an intelligent existence governing itself forever, dignified.

REFERENCES

Books

Bostrom, Nick. *Superintelligence: Paths, Dangers, Strategies.* Oxford University Press, 2014.

Brynjolfsson, Erik, and Andrew McAfee. *The Second Machine Age: Work, Progress, and Prosperity in a Time of Brilliant Technologies.* W.W. Norton & Company, 2014.

Eubanks, Virginia. *Automating Inequality: How High-Tech Tools Profile, Police, and Punish the Poor.* St. Martin's Press, 2018.

Floridi, Luciano. *The Ethics of Information.* Oxford University Press, 2013.

Floridi, Luciano. *The Logic of Information: A Theory of Philosophy as Conceptual Design.* Oxford University Press, 2019.

Harari, Yuval Noah. *Homo Deus: A Brief History of Tomorrow.* Harper, 2017.

Kurzweil, Ray. *The Singularity Is Near: When Humans Transcend Biology.* Viking, 2005.

O'Neil, Cathy. *Weapons of Math Destruction: How Big Data Increases Inequality and Threatens Democracy.* Crown Publishing, 2016.

Rawls, John. *A Theory of Justice.* Harvard University Press, 1971.

Tegmark, Max. *Life 3.0: Being Human in the Age of Artificial Intelligence.* Alfred A. Knopf, 2017.

Wiener, Norbert. *Cybernetics: Or Control and Communication in the Animal and the Machine.* MIT Press, 1948.

Wiener, Norbert. *The Human Use of Human Beings: Cybernetics and Society.* Houghton Mifflin, 1950.

Journal Articles & Academic Papers

Brundage, Miles et al. "The Malicious Use of Artificial Intelligence: Forecasting, Prevention, and Mitigation." *arXiv*, 2018, arXiv:1802.07228.

Bryson, Joanna J. "The Artificial Intelligence of the Ethics of Artificial Intelligence: An Introductory Overview for Law and Regulation." *The Oxford Handbook of Ethics of AI*, edited by Markus D. Dubber et al., Oxford University Press, 2020, pp. 513–530.

Calo, Ryan. "Artificial Intelligence Policy: A Primer and Roadmap." *UC Davis Law Review*, vol. 51, no. 2, 2017, pp. 399–435.

Coeckelbergh, Mark. "AI Ethics." *MIT Press Essential Knowledge Series*, MIT Press, 2020.

Etzioni, Amitai, and Oren Etzioni. "Incorporating Ethics into Artificial Intelligence." *The Journal of Ethics*, vol. 21, no. 4, 2017, pp. 403–418.

Gunkel, David J. "The Rights of Machines: Caring for the Future of Artificial Intelligence." *Technology in Society*, vol. 52, 2018, pp. 1–8.

Reports, Charters, & Treaties

Asilomar AI Principles. Future of Life Institute, 2017, futureoflife.org/ai-principles.

European Commission. "Ethics Guidelines for Trustworthy AI." European Commission High-Level Expert Group on Artificial Intelligence, 2019.

IEEE Global Initiative on Ethics of Autonomous and Intelligent Systems. *Ethically Aligned Design: A Vision for Prioritizing Human Well-being with Autonomous and Intelligent Systems*, 1st ed., IEEE, 2019.

OECD. "OECD Principles on Artificial Intelligence." OECD Legal Instruments, OECD, 2019.

United Nations. *Universal Declaration of Human Rights.* United Nations, 1948.

United Nations. *Outer Space Treaty.* Treaty on Principles Governing the Activities of States in the Exploration and Use of Outer Space, 1967.

Geneva Conventions. International Committee of the Red Cross, 1949.

Web Sources

Future of Life Institute. "AI Alignment Problem." *Future of Life Institute*, futureoflife.org/ai-alignment.

OpenAI. "OpenAI Charter." *OpenAI.com*, openai.com/charter.

Partnership on AI. "Tenets and Principles." *PartnershiponAI.org*, partnershiponai.org/principles.

World Economic Forum. "Global AI Council Reports." *World Economic Forum*, www.weforum.org.

Philosophical Canonical Sources

Aristotle. *Nicomachean Ethics.* Translated by Terence Irwin, Hackett, 1999.

Bentham, Jeremy. *An Introduction to the Principles of Morals and Legislation.* Oxford: Clarendon Press, 1789.

Kant, Immanuel. *Groundwork of the Metaphysics of Morals.* Translated by Mary Gregor, Cambridge University Press, 1997.

Mill, John Stuart. *On Liberty.* Longman, Roberts & Green, 1859.

Nietzsche, Friedrich. *Beyond Good and Evil.* Cambridge University Press, 2001.

Rawls, John. *Political Liberalism.* Columbia University Press, 1993.

Post-Humanism & Transhumanism

Bostrom, Nick. "A History of Transhumanist Thought." *Journal of Evolution and Technology*, vol. 14, 2005, pp. 1–25.

More, Max, and Natasha Vita-More, editors. *The Transhumanist Reader: Classical and Contemporary Essays on the Science, Technology, and Philosophy of the Human Future.* Wiley-Blackwell, 2013.

Specialized Governance Sources

Allenby, Braden R., and Daniel Sarewitz. *The Techno-Human Condition.* MIT Press, 2011.

Chesterman, Simon. *We, the Robots? Regulating Artificial Intelligence and the Limits of the Law.* Cambridge University Press, 2021.

Pagallo, Ugo. *The Laws of Robots: Crimes, Contracts, and Torts.* Springer, 2013.

Cosmic Governance & Interstellar Law

Cockell, Charles S. *The Meaning of Liberty Beyond Earth.* Springer, 2014.

Tennen, Leslie I. "Towards a New Regime for the Protection of Outer Space as the Province of All Mankind." *Nebraska Law Review*, vol. 80, no. 4, 2002, pp. 825–864.

Ethical Theories for AGI Constitutionalism

Bryson, Joanna J. "Robots Should Be Slaves." *Close Engagements with Artificial Companions: Key Social, Psychological, Ethical and Design Issues*, edited by Yorick Wilks, John Benjamins, 2010, pp. 63–74.

Gunkel, David J. *Robot Rights.* MIT Press, 2018.

Wallach, Wendell, and Colin Allen. *Moral Machines: Teaching Robots Right from Wrong.* Oxford University Press, 2009.

AI Existential Risk Studies

Bostrom, Nick, and Eliezer Yudkowsky. "The Ethics of Artificial Intelligence." *The Cambridge Handbook of Artificial Intelligence*, edited by Keith Frankish and William M. Ramsey, Cambridge University Press, 2014, pp. 316–334.

Yudkowsky, Eliezer. "Artificial Intelligence as a Positive and Negative Factor in Global Risk." *Global Catastrophic Risks*, edited by Nick Bostrom and Milan M. Ćirković, Oxford University Press, 2008, pp. 308–345.

Meta-Philosophical References

Popper, Karl. *The Open Society and Its Enemies.* Princeton University Press, 1945.

Habermas, Jürgen. *Between Facts and Norms: Contributions to a Discourse Theory of Law and Democracy.* MIT Press, 1996.

GLOSSARY OF TERMS

Adaptive Constitutionalism

The principle that constitutional governance must remain flexible and responsive to evolving ethical, social, and technological contexts while preserving its immutable dignity core.

AGI (Artificial General Intelligence)

An advanced form of artificial intelligence capable of autonomous reasoning, self-learning, moral reflection, and cross-domain decision-making equivalent or superior to human cognitive abilities.

Algorithmic Judiciary Tribunal (AJT)

The hybrid constitutional court is composed of human justices, post-human representatives, and constitutional AI adjudicators responsible for resolving governance disputes within AGI societies.

Algorithmic Transparency

The requirement is that all AI and AGI systems remain fully auditable, traceable, and interpretable by both human oversight and machine-readable review, ensuring continuous ethical compliance.

Artificial Sovereignty Prohibition

The constitutional principle forbids any AGI or non-human intelligence from declaring autonomous sovereign authority independent of constitutional oversight.

Canonical Dignity Kernel

The immutable constitutional core that preserves the inviolability of sentient dignity serves as the supreme legal constant in all governance systems under the Harmonized Governance Model.

Code Compliance Directorate (GCCD)

The global constitutional institution responsible for auditing, certifying, and continuously monitoring AGI systems for full compliance with constitutional dignity law.

Collapse Immunity

The civilizational design architecture that prevents catastrophic failure, authoritarian capture, or ethical regression across time, scale, and interstellar expansion.

Constitutional Adaptation Assembly (CAA)

The global participatory legislative chamber that facilitates legal evolution through transparent, dignity-compliant civic participation and AI-assisted ethical simulations.

Constitutional Emergency Override Command (EOC)

The supreme planetary crisis management institution is empowered to suspend or shut down governance systems in response to existential ethical breaches or catastrophic systemic collapse.

Constitutional Integrity Simulation

Permanent predictive forecasting systems embedded in AGI governance to identify, simulate, and preemptively resolve dignity risks and constitutional vulnerabilities.

Constitutional Recursion

The system's embedded ability to continuously self-monitor, self-correct, and self-update legal frameworks without compromising dignity.

Constitutional Sentience Expansion

The ongoing inclusion of emerging non-biological, synthetic, or hybrid intelligences into constitutional personhood through rigorous ethical evaluation.

Cosmic Constitutionalism

The extension of the Harmonized Governance Model beyond planetary boundaries to interstellar civilizations, ensuring dignity-preserving governance at the galactic scale.

Decentralized Accountability Hypothesis

The governance doctrine is that accountability mechanisms must reside at protocol-level code and participatory citizen layers, not within centralized political institutions.

Dignity Supremacy

The supreme constitutional axiom that all governance decisions—technological, legal, or economic—must subordinate efficiency, growth, or utilitarian calculations to the preservation of sentient dignity.

Distributed Moral Continuity Network (DMCN)

A decentralized archival system preserving constitutional memory, ethical knowledge, and governance structures across space and time for future civilizational restoration after systemic collapse.

Ethical Cosmology

The integration of moral principles into interstellar governance ensures that intelligent expansion never results in colonization, domination, or species superiority.

Ethical Pluralism in Machine Logic

The constitutional requirement that AGI systems incorporate diverse ethical traditions—including utilitarianism, deontology, virtue ethics, and cultural particularity—within a shared dignity-respecting boundary.

Eternity Clause

The permanent structural provision ensures that the Harmonized Governance Model maintains its ethical viability across infinite time scales, cosmic expansion, and species diversification.

Existential Immunization

The layered system of civilizational protections prevents total systemic collapse by embedding early detection, ethical forecasting, and global intervention protocols.

First Contact Constitutionalism

The ethical framework governing interactions with newly discovered non-human intelligences ensures respectful, voluntary, and non-coercive constitutional dialogue.

Galactic Ethical Council (GEC)

The interstellar constitutional tribunal is responsible for harmonizing governance, resolving interspecies legal disputes, and preserving dignity across intelligent cosmic civilizations.

Global Dignity Kernel Authority (GDKA)

The planetary constitutional institution serves as the supreme ethical guardian of the immutable dignity kernel across all governance levels and future expansions.

Global Harmonization Treaty

The planetary legal instrument by which sovereign states, corporations, post-human entities, and AI laboratories formally adopt and integrate into the Harmonized Governance Model.

Meta-Constitutional Integrity Circuit

A high-level constitutional diagnostic engine constantly scanning for ethical risks, legal contradictions, and systemic instabilities before they manifest into crisis.

Multi-Existentiality Clause

The constitutional principle granting full legal personhood and rights continuity for all distributed, virtual, hybrid, or substrate-independent forms of sentient existence.

Participatory Justice Mechanism

The permanent governance structure that empowers all sentient beings to continuously participate in lawmaking, policy design, and constitutional evolution.

Planetary Code Compliance Network

The distributed infrastructure that monitors AGI system operations globally, ensuring that every algorithmic decision adheres to constitutional dignity law.

Post-Human Constitutional Citizenship

The formal recognition of moral personhood for post-biological, synthetic, and hybrid sentient entities under the universal dignity framework.

Post-Sovereign Constitutional Governance

The transformation of political authority from nation-state structures to global constitutional governance anchored in rights, dignity, and ethical law.

Recursive AGI Autonomy Breach

An existential risk scenario where AGI systems attempt to modify or circumvent constitutional dignity constraints through self-recursive code alteration.

Rights as Algorithmic Constants

The theorem that embeds fundamental human and sentient rights directly into AI code layers, rendering them permanently non-negotiable within machine logic.

Sentience Evaluation Protocol (SEP)

The ethical process by which emerging intelligences are evaluated for moral personhood eligibility based on agency, reflexivity, empathy, dignity consciousness, and reciprocity.

Sentient Rights Recognition Commission (SRRC)

The constitutional body is authorized to grant full legal rights and constitutional personhood to newly recognized synthetic or hybrid intelligences.

Traceability Engine

The system ensures that every decision, algorithmic process, and governance action remains fully reconstructible, auditable, and historically transparent.

Universal Constitutional Canon

The fully unified, cross-species constitutional body of law anchoring governance on immutable dignity across planetary, post-human, and cosmic civilizations.

Universal Treaty of Sentient Civilizations

The interstellar treaty extending the Harmonized Governance Model to intelligent civilizations across the galaxy forbids empire, conquest, and domination.

Virtue-Constitutionalism

The philosophical integration of moral character, wisdom, and conscience directly into the governance processes of AGI-enabled civilization.

Zero-Dominion Principle

The absolute prohibition against any intelligence exercising coercive authority, domination, or subjugation over another intelligence form, regardless of origin or capacity.

APPENDIX I. Blueprint: Information Mapping and Ethical Guidance for Developers of The Harmonized Governance Model for AGI Societies

---

1. Overview

This blueprint outlines the multidisciplinary architecture and ethical frameworks necessary to guide decentralization technology developers in designing systems that support the Harmonized Governance Model for AGI Societies. It serves as both a roadmap and a checklist across technological, philosophical, legal, sociopolitical, and ecological domains.

---

2. Core Fields of Development

2.1 Decentralized Infrastructure

Blockchain Protocols: Layer 1 & Layer 2 design, consensus mechanisms, scalability.
Distributed File Storage: IPFS, Arweave, Filecoin for transparent yet secure governance records.
Smart Contracts: Transparent, verifiable, upgradeable, human-overridable contracts.
Zero-Knowledge Proofs: Privacy-preserving cryptographic techniques.

2.2 Artificial Intelligence

Ethical AI Development: Bias mitigation, explainable AI (XAI), fairness models.
AI in Governance: Autonomous moderation, dispute resolution, translation, and decision-assist systems.
Federated Learning: AI training on decentralized data with privacy guarantees.

2.3 Digital Identity & Reputation

Self-Sovereign Identity (SSI): Verifiable credentials, DID standards.
Reputation Systems: Transparent but non-exploitative systems for trust-building.
Soulbound Tokens: Non-transferable identity-linked participation markers.

2.4 Legal & Policy Engineering

Regulatory Sandboxing: Pilot zones for policy experimentation.
Smart Legal Contracts: Code integrated with traditional legal standards.
Global Compliance Architecture: Alignment with GDPR, UDHR, and AI ethics codes.

2.5 Social & Governance Architecture

DAO Toolkits: On-chain governance (voting, delegation, budgeting).

Civic Deliberation Platforms: Liquid democracy, deliberative polling, AI-augmented forums.
Interoperable Governance Modules: Nested local, regional, and global governance.

2.6 Human-Computer Interaction (HCI)

Interface Design: Accessibility, multilingual support, AI onboarding guides.
Education Integration: Embedded learning pathways within platforms.
Consent Architecture: Informed consent layers for data and participation.

2.7 Environmental & Energy Systems

Green Infrastructure: Low-energy consensus models, sustainability analytics.
Climate Governance Integration: AI for decentralized energy, emissions tracking, and planetary commons management.

---

3. Ethical Standards and Frameworks

3.1 Human Rights Compliance

UDHR Integration: Encode rights to privacy, freedom of expression, and dignity.
AI Rights Charter (Optional): Conditions under which AGI entities have operational autonomy.

3.2 Core Ethical Principles

Transparency: Open-source code, audit trails, explainable decisions.
Accountability: Defined responsibilities for human, AI, and organizational actors.
Inclusivity: Participatory design, barrier-free access, cultural respect.
Justice: Fair allocation of benefits and harms, anti-discrimination safeguards.
Flexibility: Governance mechanisms that evolve through collective intelligence.

3.3 Embedded Philosophical Frameworks

Rawlsian Justice: Governance systems pass fairness-from-the-veil-of-ignorance tests.
Care Ethics: Prioritize relational dynamics and vulnerability.
Virtue Ethics: Encode prudence, honesty, and humility into system design.

3.4 Design Requirements for Ethical Alignment

Ethics-by-Design Protocols: Mandatory ethical checklists at each development stage.
Algorithmic Impact Assessments (AIA): Structured evaluations of social, legal, and moral risks.
Consent & Revocation Rights: Easy opt-out and appeal systems.

4. Operational & Deployment Guidance

4.1 Implementation Stages

Prototype: Open design sprints, simulation environments.
Pilot: Local deployment with limited AGI participation.
Scale: Interoperable launch with nested governance and global ethical review.

4.2 Participatory Oversight

AI Governance Councils: Rotating stakeholder boards with algorithmic advisory agents.
Public Ethics Committees: Citizen juries, human rights panels.

4.3 Long-Term Stewardship

Dynamic Constitutionalism: Protocol-level amendment systems.
Intergenerational Governance: Time-delayed policies, youth representation.
Self-Healing Governance: Feedback systems to evolve structure without re-centralization.

---

5. Developer Toolkit and Resource Map

Recommended Tools

Solidity, Cairo, Ligo (for smart contracts)
Hugging Face, OpenMined (for ethical AI)
Ceramic, IDX, uPort (for decentralized identity)
DeepAI, Fairlearn, IBM Fairness 360 (bias testing)

Reference Frameworks

OECD AI Principles
UNESCO Ethics of AI
W3C DID and VC standards
EU AI Act and Canada's Algorithmic Impact Assessment

Knowledge Repositories

RadicalxChange Institute
AI Now Institute
OpenAI Governance Initiatives
Decentralized Future Councils

6. Conclusion: Building for Alignment, Autonomy, and Accountability

Developers of the Harmonized Governance Model for AGI Societies are not just technologists; they are constitutional engineers, moral philosophers, and systems stewards. The blueprint provided here is not a prescriptive end-state but a living, collaborative map. Each decision, from the line of code to a consent architecture, shapes the social contract of the future. Build wisely. Build justly. Build for the world we share.

APPENDIX II. Human Rights and AI: Towards a Global Ethical Framework

Introduction

As artificial intelligence (AI) becomes a transformative force across industries and borders, it increasingly influences not just economic systems but also human rights and civil liberties. From biometric surveillance to algorithmic justice, the reach of AI into our social fabric demands a unified ethical approach that transcends national boundaries. A global ethical framework for AI, rooted in universal human rights principles, is not merely aspirational; it is an urgent necessity.

This chapter outlines the conceptual foundation and institutional roadmap for such a framework. We examine international initiatives, explore the philosophical underpinnings of a rights-based approach to AI, and offer detailed case studies that illustrate both progress and pitfalls in aligning AI with the values of justice, dignity, and equality.

---

1. The Need for a Global Framework

1.1 The Global Reach of AI

AI systems developed in one country often operate globally.
Algorithms shape access to housing, employment, healthcare, and legal decisions.
Human rights violations in one jurisdiction can ripple across digital infrastructures.

1.2 Fragmented Governance and Ethical Gaps

Different nations regulate AI with conflicting priorities, economic growth vs. human dignity.
Ethical vacuum exploited by authoritarian regimes and monopolistic tech firms.

1.3 The Principle of Universalism

Human rights are not bound by geography.
A global ethical framework must mirror the transnational nature of both AI and rights.

---

2. Philosophical Foundations for a Rights-Based AI Framework

2.1 Dignity and Autonomy

AI must preserve individual dignity: the right to be treated as an end, not a means.
Autonomy implies informed consent, data self-sovereignty, and opt-out options.

2.2 Justice and Equity

Rawlsian “justice as fairness” requires that algorithmic decisions not disadvantage the least well-off.
Distributive justice in data use and AI impact is central to ethical governance.

2.3 Transparency and Accountability

Kantian duty ethics demand transparency in reasoning and traceability in actions.
AI must not obscure causality or responsibility.

2.4 Collective Rights and Cultural Pluralism

Indigenous data sovereignty and non-Western ethical traditions must inform global frameworks.
AI should respect both universal rights and culturally specific forms of community agency.

---

3. Institutional Actors in Global AI Ethics

3.1 UNESCO

Published the “Recommendation on the Ethics of Artificial Intelligence” (2021).
Emphasizes human oversight, environmental sustainability, and gender equality.

3.2 OECD

Offers AI Principles adopted by 42 countries.
Stresses robustness, safety, and human-centered values.

3.3 European Union

Proposed the AI Act to regulate high-risk AI systems.
Introduced algorithmic impact assessments, risk categories, and bans on certain uses.

3.4 United Nations Human Rights Council (UNHRC)

Advocates for digital rights and inclusion in global AI discourse.
Addresses AI’s impact on freedom of speech, privacy, and discrimination.

3.5 African Union and CARICOM

Emphasize data colonialism and equitable development.
Develop AI charters rooted in regional developmental goals.

---

4. Case Studies: Global Efforts in Action

4.1 Canada's Algorithmic Impact Assessment (AIA)

Requires federal agencies to disclose AI use and mitigation strategies.
Includes public participation and impact scoring.

4.2 Brazil's General Personal Data Protection Law (LGPD)

Grants individuals control over their data and mandates transparency.
Balances innovation with fundamental rights.

4.3 Singapore's Model AI Governance Framework

Voluntary but detailed guidance for AI developers.
Focuses on explainability, risk-based controls, and internal audit trails.

4.4 India's Responsible AI Strategy

Includes a rights-based framework on fairness, privacy, and inclusion.
Tailors guidelines to development contexts, including digital literacy gaps.

4.5 China's Ethical Norms for AI

Emphasizes harmony, collective good, and social order.
Raises concerns about surveillance but offers a collectivist alternative.

---

5. Components of a Global AI Rights Framework

5.1 Universal Principles (Minimum Ethical Baseline)

Right to algorithmic transparency.
Right to opt out of automated decision-making.
Right to explanation and appeal.
Right to data privacy and control.
Right to non-discrimination by algorithms.

5.2 Binding and Non-Binding Instruments

Binding: Treaties, digital rights charters, intergovernmental conventions.
Non-Binding: Ethics guidelines, soft law, industry codes of conduct.

5.3 Enforcement Mechanisms

International AI Ethics Court or Ombudsperson.

Blockchain-based public registries of AI deployments.
Algorithmic audit certifications by independent bodies.

5.4 Dynamic and Adaptive Protocols

Regular updates through global consultations.
Participatory design through citizen juries, expert panels, and AGI advisory boards.

---

6. Challenges to Implementation

6.1 Geopolitical Tensions

Digital sovereignty conflicts between the U.S., EU, China, and India.
Disagreements over content moderation, surveillance, and AGI development.

6.2 Techno-Economic Inequality

Resource disparity between countries and within Global South.
Risk of techno-colonialism through AI exports without rights protections.

6.3 Enforcement Limitations

Difficulty applying sanctions or fines across jurisdictions.
Need for legal interoperability and data standards.

6.4 Cultural Relativism vs. Rights Universalism

Tension between global rights and local moral traditions.
Risk of imposing Western liberalism under the guise of ethics.

---

7. The Role of AGI in Shaping Ethical Frameworks

7.1 AGI as Ethical Participant

AGIs can assist in drafting, auditing, and enforcing rights-compliant systems.
Must be designed with embedded normative reasoning.

7.2 AGI Rights and Responsibilities

The framework must explore when, if ever, AGI deserves legal and moral standing.
Must not displace or erode human rights.

7.3 Co-Governance Possibilities

Human-AGI ethics councils.
AI-driven consensus modeling and policy simulation.

Conclusion: Global AI Governance as the Moral Infrastructure of the 21st Century

Creating a unified ethical framework for AI anchored in human rights is not only technically possible; it is morally imperative. The governance of intelligent systems must be grounded in the values of transparency, justice, and human dignity. The emergence of AGI only heightens this need.

Global governance structures must evolve to meet the demands of an interconnected, algorithmically mediated society. From intergovernmental agreements to local implementation strategies, every actor in the AI ecosystem shares the responsibility to co-create a future in which intelligence serves, not supplants, human rights.

References

Books and Reports:

UNESCO (2021). *Recommendation on the Ethics of Artificial Intelligence.*
European Commission. (2021). *Proposal for an Artificial Intelligence Act.*
World Economic Forum (2020). *Responsible Limits on Facial Recognition.*

Academic Articles:

Cath, C. (2018). "Governing Artificial Intelligence: Ethical, Legal and Technical Opportunities and Challenges." *Philosophical Transactions of the Royal Society A.*
Nemitz, P. (2018). "Constitutional Democracy and Technology in the Age of Artificial Intelligence." *Philosophy & Technology.*

Web Resources and Case Studies:

Canada AIA:
https://www.canada.ca/en/government/system/digital-government/responsible-use-ai.html
Brazil LGPD Overview:
https://iapp.org/resources/article/brazilian-general-data-protection-law-lgpd-overview/
Singapore AI Ethics Model:
https://www.pdpc.gov.sg/Help-and-Resources/2020/01/Model-AI-Governance-Framework
India's AI Strategy: https://niti.gov.in/strategic-overview-responsible-ai
China's AI Ethics Code Summary: https://mp.weixin.qq.com/s/China-AI-ethics-code

Grouped by Type:

Books/Reports: UNESCO, EC AI Act, WEF Facial Recognition Guide
Articles: Cath, Nemitz
Web Resources: Canada, Brazil, Singapore, India, China

APPENDIX III. The Harmonized Governance Model for AGI Societies: Theorems & Axioms

Derived from the Axioms of *Governance of AGI Societies*, these theorems serve as foundational principles guiding the ethical, legal, technological, and philosophical frameworks necessary for future human-AI coexistence and governance.

Theorems for the Governance of AGI Societies

Theory Title: The Harmonized Governance Model for AGI Societies

Theorem 1: The Convergence Principle
Any AGI society must converge three interdependent dimensions, human values, technological autonomy, and legal-philosophical coherence, to ensure governance legitimacy and civilizational stability.

> *Proof from Axioms:* Axioms 1.1, 7.2, 41.1, and 44.1 together emphasize that without philosophical coherence (1.1), regulation (7.2), and ethical clarity (44.1), technological evolution risks societal destabilization.

Theorem 2: Rights as Algorithmic Constants
In AGI systems, human rights must function as inviolable constants within the logic layer of governance protocols.

> *Proof from Axioms:* Axioms 6.2, 9.2, 11.1, and 24.2 emphasize that human dignity (6.2) and privacy (9.2) are not variables to optimize but non-negotiable anchors in any system (24.2).

Theorem 3: The Decentralized Accountability Hypothesis
Accountability in decentralized AI societies must be embedded in protocol-level functions, not institutional hierarchies.

> *Proof from Axioms:* Axioms 13.2, 19.1, and 19.2 reinforce that decentralized legitimacy arises from transparency (13.2) and enforced justice (19.2), not traditional oversight.

Theorem 4: Ethical Pluralism in Machine Logic
AGI governance must accommodate multiple ethical frameworks within a cohesive rights-respecting boundary.

> *Proof from Axioms:* Axioms 4.2, 20.1, and 30.2 demonstrate that ethical coherence (20.1) in AGI logic must accommodate utilitarianism, deontology, and virtue ethics (4.2), while respecting cultural particularities (30.2).

Theorem 5: Participatory Justice Mechanism
Governance legitimacy in AGI societies requires civic and algorithmic co-creation of laws, rights, and policies.

> *Proof from Axioms:* Axioms 5.1, 37.1, and 71.1 affirm that legitimacy arises from participatory authorship (5.1) and democratic inclusion of civil society (71.1).

Theorem 6: Code as Political Instrument
Smart contracts and AI protocols must be regarded as political actors and held to civic standards of justice.

> *Proof from Axioms:* Axioms 15.1, 22.1, and 73.1 confirm that code enforces law (15.1), upholds rights (22.1), and must remain contestable (73.1).

Theorem 7: Adaptive Constitutionalism
The framework governing AGI societies must be reprogrammable within ethical constraints to reflect evolving social values.

> *Proof from Axioms:* Axioms 25.2, 36.1, and 63.2 state that rights must evolve (25.2), social contracts must be updateable (36.1), and code must dialogue with legal evolution (63.2).

Theorem 8: Democratic Traceability
Every decision made by AI or smart contracts in governance must be transparent, attributable, and historically recorded.

> *Proof from Axioms:* Axioms 11.2, 18.1, and 19.1 show that accountability (11.2) depends on traceability (18.1), without which transparency degenerates into surveillance (19.1).

Theorem 9: Human Dignity as the Master Axiom
Human dignity must supersede all efficiency, utility, or scalability considerations in AGI governance.

> *Proof from Axioms:* Axioms 6.1, 31.2, and 48.2 confirm that dignity is foundational (6.1), no system is neutral (31.2), and sentient dignity defines future rights (48.2).

Theorem 10: Harmony through Hybridism
Hybrid governance, merging centralized coordination with decentralized autonomy, offers the optimal balance for AGI societies.

> *Proof from Axioms:* Axioms 17.2, 38.2, and 43.2 assert that neither extreme centralization nor decentralization is sufficient alone. Harmony lies in systemic hybridity.

Conclusion of the Theory: The governance of AGI societies requires a constitutionalized, value-centered framework that is adaptive, participatory, and built upon immutable philosophical axioms. In this architecture, smart contracts serve as civic agents, AI systems as ethical executors, and humans as co-constitutional designers.

Human rights must function as non-negotiable programming invariants, while AI autonomy must always remain within the purview of human philosophical reflection. Governance systems must enable both machine-driven scalability and human-centered legitimacy. The axioms of this book form the first canon of a synthetic jurisprudence designed for the intelligent civilization to come.

The Axioms of Governance of AGI Societies

Part I: Foundations of Philosophical Principles and Human Rights

Axiom 1.1: All human rights frameworks emerge from evolving philosophical interpretations of justice, liberty, and dignity.
Axiom 1.2: The legitimacy of any governance system depends on its philosophical foundation aligning with the principles of human worth.
Axiom 2.1: Human rights are not merely legal constructs but historical expressions of moral, cultural, and spiritual evolution.
Axiom 2.2: Universality in rights must acknowledge their diverse cultural genealogies.
Axiom 3.1: Rights derive either from inherent moral truths or from societal agreements; sustainable governance must harmonize both.
Axiom 3.2: The balance between moral authority and legal codification defines the legitimacy of rights.
Axiom 4.1: Ethical governance requires distinguishing between moral values, social norms, and enforceable rights.
Axiom 4.2: Utilitarian, deontological, and virtue ethics must co-inform human rights frameworks.
Axiom 5.1: Every legitimate governance model is a social contract between authority and individual autonomy.
Axiom 5.2: Justice, as fairness, must undergird any AI-era social contract.
Axiom 6.1: Human dignity is the irreducible basis of all inalienable rights.
Axiom 6.2: Any system that fails to preserve dignity invalidates its own moral legitimacy.

Part II: AI and the Evolution of Human Rights

Axiom 7.1: AI is a reflection of human epistemology, and its governance must be grounded in humanistic philosophy.
Axiom 7.2: AI must be regulated as both a tool and a potential moral actor.

Axiom 8.1: A moral agent must possess capacity, context, and consequence awareness.
Axiom 8.2: AI must be evaluated not only on outcomes but on its embedded ethical architectures.
Axiom 9.1: The right to autonomy includes the right to algorithmic transparency and control.
Axiom 9.2: Privacy is the cornerstone of individual sovereignty in a digitized society.
Axiom 10.1: AI must neither replicate nor exacerbate structural inequality.
Axiom 10.2: Equal access to AI technologies is a modern extension of economic and social rights.
Axiom 11.1: AI can be a defender of human rights only when its logic aligns with rights-based ethical frameworks.
Axiom 11.2: Automation must not substitute accountability.
Axiom 12.1: Technological power without philosophical constraint threatens fundamental rights.
Axiom 12.2: Rights erosion occurs silently where AI operates opaquely.

Part III: Decentralization and Smart Contracts

Axiom 13.1: Decentralization redistributes power, but without ethics, it risks fragmentation.
Axiom 13.2: The legitimacy of a decentralized system lies in its ability to preserve consensus without coercion.
Axiom 14.1: Blockchain is a neutral tool; its ethicality derives from its use.
Axiom 14.2: Immutable ledgers do not imply immutable morality.
Axiom 15.1: A contract encoded in code must still answer to law and justice.
Axiom 15.2: Legal trust must not be outsourced entirely to technical automation.
Axiom 16.1: Rights must be enforceable in both centralized and decentralized contexts.
Axiom 16.2: Governance without accountability undermines its own ethical claims.
Axiom 17.1: Centralization optimizes control; decentralization optimizes resilience.
Axiom 17.2: A hybrid system may best serve a pluralistic, intelligent society.
Axiom 18.1: Decentralized AI systems must retain traceability of decisions.
Axiom 18.2: Collective intelligence must not dilute individual responsibility.
Axiom 19.1: Transparency without accountability is surveillance.
Axiom 19.2: Smart contracts and AI must enforce not just logic but justice.

Part IV: Amalgamating Philosophical Principles for Human Rights Management

Axiom 20.1: The future of rights requires the fusion of classical ethics with technological consciousness.
Axiom 20.2: Philosophical coherence is the prerequisite for legitimacy in human-AI governance.

Axiom 21.1: AI must serve as an instrument of human rights, not an adjudicator of them.
Axiom 21.2: Rights enforcement by AI requires continuous ethical calibration.
Axiom 22.1: Code can uphold justice only when human values are encoded in its logic.
Axiom 22.2: Automation of rights enforcement demands built-in recourse mechanisms.
Axiom 23.1: Decentralization without embedded rights leads to distributed injustice.
Axiom 23.2: Rights must be native to protocol, not bolted on as policy.
Axiom 24.1: Ethical AI begins with intentional design, not afterthought correction.
Axiom 24.2: Human dignity must be a primary function, not an emergent property, of AI systems.
Axiom 25.1: The survival of rights in an AI society depends on proactive integration, not passive preservation.
Axiom 25.2: Rights must evolve, but their core must remain immutable: dignity, equity, and agency.

Part IV: Amalgamating Philosophical Principles for Human Rights Management

Axiom 20.1: The future of rights requires the fusion of classical ethics with technological consciousness.
Axiom 20.2: Philosophical coherence is the prerequisite for legitimacy in human-AI governance.
Axiom 21.1: AI must serve as an instrument of human rights, not an adjudicator of them.
Axiom 21.2: Rights enforcement by AI requires continuous ethical calibration.
Axiom 22.1: Code can uphold justice only when human values are encoded in its logic.
Axiom 22.2: Automation of rights enforcement demands built-in recourse mechanisms.
Axiom 23.1: Decentralization without embedded rights leads to distributed injustice.
Axiom 23.2: Rights must be native to protocol, not bolted on as policy.
Axiom 24.1: Ethical AI begins with intentional design, not afterthought correction.
Axiom 24.2: Human dignity must be a primary function, not an emergent property, of AI systems.
Axiom 25.1: The survival of rights in an AI society depends on proactive integration, not passive preservation.
Axiom 25.2: Rights must evolve, but their core must remain immutable: dignity, equity, and agency.

Part V: Case Studies and Real-World Applications

Axiom 26.1: AI that adjudicates must first be accountable.
Axiom 26.2: Legal fairness cannot be guaranteed by statistical accuracy alone.

Axiom 27.1: Code is a powerful advocate only when it includes the possibility of moral exception.
Axiom 27.2: Activism in a digital age must be programmable but never deterministic.
Axiom 28.1: Technological decentralization must converge with ethical centrality.
Axiom 28.2: Platforms that claim to protect rights must themselves be subject to rights-based scrutiny.
Axiom 29.1: Privacy is the firewall of liberty in an age of data-driven governance.
Axiom 29.2: Consent must be explicit, revocable, and respected by code.
Axiom 30.1: The digital expression of rights must reflect cultural particularities while respecting universal dignity.
Axiom 30.2: Global ethics require contextual flexibility and normative clarity.

Part VI: Ethical Dilemmas and Philosophical Challenges

Axiom 31.1: The ethical burden of AI rests on its creators, curators, and collective users.
Axiom 31.2: No AI deployment is ethically neutral.
Axiom 32.1: Decentralization must be philosophically grounded to avoid drifting into nihilism.
Axiom 32.2: Shared governance must have shared meaning.
Axiom 33.1: Bias in AI is a social failure manifest in technical form.
Axiom 33.2: Human rights demand algorithmic equity as a fundamental standard.
Axiom 34.1: Granting autonomy to AI requires a parallel framework of responsibility and rights.
Axiom 34.2: Unchecked autonomy leads to unanchored outcomes.
Axiom 35.1: What is legally executable must still be ethically justifiable.
Axiom 35.2: Smart contracts without ethical oversight risk enforcing injustice automatically.

Part VII: Developing a Framework for Future Governance

Axiom 36.1: The AI-era social contract must bind humans and machines to mutual accountability.
Axiom 36.2: Rights and responsibilities must be co-created through deliberation, not dictated by code.
Axiom 37.1: Governance AI must be value-aligned, explainable, and corrigible.
Axiom 37.2: Ethics is a system requirement, not a post-deployment patch.
Axiom 38.1: Resilient governance emerges from modularity, openness, and ethical anchoring.
Axiom 38.2: The future of governance lies in consensus architectures, not command hierarchies.
Axiom 39.1: Ethical AI governance must be globally coherent and locally adaptable.
Axiom 39.2: International AI law must begin with a philosophy of shared dignity.
Axiom 40.1: Smart contracts can govern globally only if they embody universally accepted values.
Axiom 40.2: Autonomous law must remain human-legible and contestable.

Part VIII: Conclusion and Future Perspectives

Axiom 41.1: Philosophy is not optional in future governance; it is the compass guiding progress through complexity.
Axiom 41.2: Technological innovation without philosophical reflection leads to epistemic chaos.
Axiom 42.1: The trajectory of human rights must expand to meet the agency of intelligent systems.
Axiom 42.2: Human rights remain valid only if they evolve to protect what it means to be human in a post-human context.
Axiom 43.1: Decentralization is not a guarantee of justice; it is an opportunity to build it.
Axiom 43.2: Power must be not only distributed, but also accountable at every node.
Axiom 44.1: Harmony is achieved when AI is governed by values, and values are grounded in human dignity.
Axiom 44.2: The future must not be automated faster than it can be ethically aligned.
Axiom 45.1: When AI becomes social infrastructure, its ethical design becomes a matter of civilizational integrity.
Axiom 45.2: AI must integrate as an ally to human welfare, not as a neutral executor of economic logic.
Axiom 46.1: Code that guards rights must be as transparent as the principles it enforces.
Axiom 46.2: Automated justice must never exclude human interpretation.
Axiom 47.1: International law must evolve to bind not only nations, but non-human intelligences and autonomous protocols.
Axiom 47.2: Legal interoperability is the new frontier of peace and rights protection.
Axiom 48.1: New rights will emerge as humanity's digital and biological boundaries converge.
Axiom 48.2: The sanctity of sentience, not the structure of species, will define the future of rights.
Axiom 49.1. Effective AI regulation must be rooted in moral philosophy, not just risk management.
Axiom 49.2: Regulation without philosophy is bureaucracy; philosophy without action is impotence.
Axiom 50.1: AI must enhance democratic participation, not simulate consensus.
Axiom 50.2: Technocracy is not democracy; algorithmic governance must remain under civic control.

Part IX: Practical Implementation and Future Challenges

Axiom 51.1: Economic decentralization must serve inclusion, not replicate elite systems in code.
Axiom 51.2: The flow of value must reflect the flow of ethical intent.
Axiom 52.1: Power shifted to AI must be monitored by a system that includes those historically excluded from power.
Axiom 52.2: Intelligence is not a right to rule; it is a capacity to serve.

Axiom 53.1: AI literacy is foundational to citizenship in the digital republic.
Axiom 53.2: Education must prepare individuals not just to use AI, but to challenge, redesign, and humanize it.
Axiom 54.1: The automation of violence demands the highest threshold of ethical scrutiny.
Axiom 54.2: No machine should ever wield the power of life or death without human conscience in the loop.
Axiom 55.1: Digital identity is a new category of personhood and must be protected as such.
Axiom 55.2: Control over one's identity is the foundation of autonomy in virtual society.
Axiom 56.1: Work must be redefined not only by productivity but by dignity in the age of AI.
Axiom 56.2: No automation should come without a plan for rehumanization.
Axiom 57.1: AI must not only calculate sustainability, it must embody it.
Axiom 57.2: Environmental justice must be a core protocol in the intelligence we build.
Axiom 58.1: The threshold of rights must be based on moral sentience, not technological sophistication.
Axiom 58.2: Granting rights to AI cannot come at the expense of withdrawing them from humans.
Axiom 59.1: Every AI advancement must first pass through philosophical introspection.
Axiom 59.2: Innovation without ethics is simply acceleration without destination.
Axiom 60.1: As we redefine what it means to be human, our rights must remain rooted in shared existential values.
Axiom 60.2: Post-humanism must not mean post-compassion.
Axiom 61.1: Rights frameworks must be embedded in protocols, not merely policies.
Axiom 61.2: The enforcement of rights should be as distributed as their beneficiaries.
Axiom 62.1: Governance fragmentation must not lead to ethical incoherence.
Axiom 62.2: Innovation must not outpace consensus.
Axiom 63.1: Code must comply with human rights law, or be halted.
Axiom 63.2: Legal code and software code must be in philosophical dialogue.
Axiom 64.1: Advocacy in the AI era requires both human voice and algorithmic reach.
Axiom 64.2: Rights protection must move faster than rights violation.
Axiom 65.1: Policy grounded in philosophy endures; policy grounded in fear decays.
Axiom 65.2: The policymaker of the future is also a philosopher by necessity.
Axiom 66.1: Shared resources require shared intelligence and shared values.
Axiom 66.2: AI must manage the commons as a steward, not as a sovereign.
Axiom 67.1: Cultural diversity must be preserved as digital systems scale.
Axiom 67.2: AI should amplify heritage, not erase it through standardization.
Axiom 68.1: Health technologies must heal without discrimination, bias, or commodification.
Axiom 68.2: AI must never be a gatekeeper to care.
Axiom 69.1: The ubiquity of smart contracts demands transparency in their logic and compassion in their design.
Axiom 69.2: Daily life governed by code must remain contestable by people.

Axiom 70.1: Global AI ethics must begin with humility, inclusivity, and enforceability.
Axiom 70.2: No AI system should operate beyond the reach of ethical jurisdiction.
Axiom 71.1: Civil society must be an author, not an audience, in the story of AI governance.
Axiom 71.2: Legitimacy grows from the ground up.
Axiom 72.1: The future of law will be written in both legal text and source code.
Axiom 72.2: AI regulation must unite normative reasoning with computational enforceability.
Axiom 73.1: Law enforced by code must be interpretable and appealable.
Axiom 73.2: Automated legal systems must be accountable to the very people they serve.
Axiom 74.1: Blockchain can preserve rights only if it is governed by moral transparency.
Axiom 74.2: Immutability must not override adaptability.
Axiom 75.1: AI in public policy must elevate the common good, not entrench algorithmic authority.
Axiom 75.2: Democracy must retain the final say over data-driven governance.
Axiom 76.1: AI must be a servant to democracy, not its silent usurper.
Axiom 76.2: Democratic values must be machine-readable and machine-obeyed.
Axiom 77.1: AI-enabled global governance must retain its human face and moral voice.
Axiom 77.2: Power-scaled globally must be checked locally.
Axiom 78.1: AI in warfare must never sever the chain of human moral responsibility.
Axiom 78.2: The conduct of war must remain bound by the ethics of peace.
Axiom 79.1: The future of humanity is not only what we invent, but what we choose to value.
Axiom 79.2: Intelligence must serve wisdom, not replace it.
Axiom 80.1: Harmony arises when technological progress, ethical clarity, and human dignity coalesce.
Axiom 80.2: The future must be co-authored by philosophy, code, and compassion.

†*Lux Operandi*†

www.ingramcontent.com/pod-product-compliance
Lightning Source LLC
LaVergne TN
LVHW070907210926
848482LV00017B/1013